ACCOUNTING

Introduction to Financial Accounting
Henry Dauderis & David Annand

Edited by Athabasca University

Version 2018 — Revision A

LYRYX WITH OPEN TEXTS

The form of this book is completely new to the Canadian market. As authors we have many years of experience in hard copy book publishing with a major international publisher. This time we are publishing an **open text** in collaboration with Lyryx Learning, supporting open content as part of their Lyryx with Open Texts products & services.

While there is no requirement that users of the book do anything more than download the pdf files and use them for non-profit educational purposes, the texts are aligned with Lyryx with Open Texts products and services offering the following benefits.

OPEN TEXT

The text can be downloaded in electronic format, printed, and can be distributed to students at no cost. Instructors who adopt Lyryx with Open Texts may obtain the relevant original text files from the authors if the instructors decide they wish to amplify certain sections for their own students. In collaboration with the authors, Lyryx will also adapt the content and provide custom editions for specific courses.

ONLINE ASSESSMENT

Lyryx has developed corresponding formative online assessment for homework and quizzes. These are genuine questions for the subject and adapted to the content. Student answers are carefully analyzed by the system and personalized feedback is immediately provided to help students improve on their work. Lyryx provides all the tools required to manage your online assessment including student grade reports and student performance statistics.

INSTRUCTOR SUPPLEMENTS

A number of resources are available, including a full set of slides for instructors and students. These are available in their original format, and consequently can be further adapted by instructors. An Exam Builder tool is also available allowing instructors to easily create paper quizzes and exams.

SUPPORT

Lyryx provides all of the support you and your students need! Starting from the course preparation time to beyond the end of the course, the Lyryx staff is available 7 days/week to provide assistance. This may include adapting the text, managing multiple sections of the course, providing course supplements, as well as timely assistance to students with registration, navigation, and daily organization.

Contact Lyryx!
info@lyryx.com

Table of Contents

Solutions To Problems

Chapter 1 Solutions

1. Generally accepted accounting principles (GAAP) are a set of principles and assumptions that guide the preparation of financial statements, and that have gained wide-spread acceptance among users and practitioners.

2. The revenue recognition principle assumes that revenue is earned by the entity at the time when a service is provided or when a sale is made, not necessarily when cash is received.

3. The matching concept states that revenue is recognized in the time period when goods and services are provided and that the assets of the entity that have been used up during the time period (expenses) must be matched with the asset inflows (revenues) during the same period.

4. Accounting information should be comparable, verifiable, timely and understandable. Accounting information should only be disclosed if it is material – that is, of sufficient size or importance to influence the judgement of a reasonably knowledgeable user. Accounting information should also be disclosed in such a manner that the benefits of doing so outweigh the costs.

5. An asset is anything of value that is owned by the entity. Assets are economic resources controlled by an entity. They have some future value to the entity, usually for generating revenue.

6. A liability is an obligation to pay an asset or to provide services or goods in the future. Until the obligations are paid, creditors have claims against the assets of the entity.

   Equity represents the amount of assets owing to the owners of the entity. The total assets of an entity belong either to the shareholders or to the creditors.

7. The exchange of assets or obligations by a business entity, expressed in monetary terms like dollars, is called a financial transaction. The exchange of cash for land or a building is an example of such a transaction.

8. The three forms of business organization are corporations, sole proprietorships, and partnerships.

9. A business entity is a unit of accountability that exists independently from other units. A set of accounting records is kept for each unit or entity. The entity exists separately from its owners. This concept is important because it keeps separate all the various activities

in which the owner is involved; lumping all the activities together would not yield useful information for keeping track of the financial performance each financial unit.

10. Financial statements evaluate the performance of an entity and measure its progress. Financial information is collected, then summarized and reported in the financial statements (balance sheet, income statement, statement of cash flows, and statement of changes in equity).

11. The date line on the income statement, statement of changes in equity, and statement of cash flows represents a period of time. The income statement details the revenues and expenses that occurred over a given period of time. The statement of changes in equity shows how equity changed over a given period of time. The statement of cash flows shows how the balance in cash changed over a given period of time. The date line on the balance sheet is a point in time because each account listed on the balance sheet identifies the account balance on a specific date.

12. The purpose of the income statement is to communicate the inflow of assets, in the form of revenues, and the outflow or consumption of assets, in the form of expenses, over a period of time. Total inflows greater than total outflows creates net income or profit, which is reported on the Income statement and in retained earnings in the equity section of the balance sheet. The purpose of the balance sheet is to communicate what the entity owns (its assets), what the entity owes (its liabilities), and the difference between assets and liabilities (its equity) at a point in time.

If revenue is recorded on the income statement, there is usually a corresponding increase in assets on the balance sheet. Similarly, if expenses are recorded on the income statement, there is generally a decrease in assets or increase of liabilities on the balance sheet.

13. Revenue is an increase in an entity's assets or a decrease in liabilities in return for services performed or goods sold, expressed in monetary units like dollars. An expense is an asset belonging to the entity that is used up or obligations incurred in selling goods or performing services.

14. Net income is the difference between revenues and expenses. It communicates whether the activities of the entity are being conducted profitably. Thus it is one measure of the success of the entity. Net income is one of the criteria used to determine the amount of dividends to be declared.

15. The statement of changes in equity shows why share capital and retained earnings have changed over a specified period of time – for instance, when shares are issued or net income is earned. The statement of cash flows explains to the users of the financial statements the entity's sources (inflows) and the uses (outflows) of cash over a specified period of time.

16. Financial statements are prepared at regular intervals to keep a number of interested groups informed about the financial performance of an entity. The timing is determined in response to the needs of management in running the entity or of outside parties, such as bankers to aid in granting loans to the entity, shareholders, or others interested in evaluating the

progress of the entity. They are generally used as a means to inform investing and lending decisions.

17. The accounting equation has the following form:

ASSETS	=	LIABILITIES	+	EQUITY
(economic resources owned by an entity)		(creditors' claims to assets)		(owners' claims to assets – residual claims)

The entity has assets, which are the resources it owns. The total assets owned by an entity must always equal the total claims of creditors and owners, who have the residual claims.

A company's accounting equation is expanded to include major categories of the balance sheet, like cash and share capital. An expanded form of the accounting equation could be as follows:

ASSETS	=	LIABILITIES	+	EQUITY
Cash+Accounts Receivable +Equipment+Truck		Accounts Payable		Share Capital +Retained Earnings

18. The double entry accounting system reflects the fact that each financial transaction affects at least two items in the accounting equation, in order to maintain the equality of the equation. For example,

   a. A truck is sold for cash: The asset truck decreases and the asset cash increases.

   b. An obligation is paid: The liability accounts payable decreases and the asset cash decreases.

   c. An account is collected: The asset cash increases and the asset accounts receivable decreases.

In this way, the equation always remains in balance after each transaction is recorded.

19. A year-end is the last day of the fiscal year of the entity. The income statement, statement of cash flows, and statement of changes in equity reflect financial translations for the year up to this date. The balance sheet reflects the financial position of the entity at the year-end date. Interim financial statements may be prepared more frequently, say quarterly or monthly; these are prepared for each entity only if required by certain users, usually shareholders of large corporations with many shareholders. Year-end financial statements must be prepared for all entities.

20. A fiscal year refers to a 12-month accounting period and that may not coincide with the calendar year. A company whose fiscal year-end coincides with the calendar year has a December 31 year-end.

Chapter 2 Solutions

1. The use of a transactions worksheet is impractical in actual practice because the record

keeping and the calculation of totals becomes convoluted. This method is therefore not very efficient or convenient, especially for a business with a high volume of transactions.

2. An *account* is an accounting record designed to classify and accumulate the dollar effect of financial transactions. In a simplified account called a T-account, the term "debit" is used to describe the left side of the account, while the term "credit" refers to the right side.

3. The association of "good" and "bad" or "increase" and "decrease" with credits and debits is not a valid association. To an accountant, "debit" means only "place an amount of the left side of an account" and "credit" means only "place an amount on the right side of an account."

4. A debit, which is always on the left side, records an increase in assets and expenses. A credit, which is always on the right side, records a decrease in assets and expenses. For example,

   a. If an asset like a truck is purchased for cash, the asset account "Truck" is debited and the Cash account is credited.

   b. If rent expense is incurred and paid with cash, the account "Rent Expense" is debited. The Cash account is credited.

5. A debit, which is always on the left side, records a decrease in liabilities, equity, and revenue. A credit, which is always on the right side, records an increase in liabilities, equity, and revenue. For example,

   a. A cash sale is made. Cash is debited, Sales is credited.

   b. We incur an expense, so we debit the expense account and credit a liability account like Accounts Payable.

   c. We issue some share capital for cash. The general ledger account Share Capital is credited and Cash is debited.

	Assets, Expenses	*Liabilities, Equity, Revenues*
6.	Increases are debited.	Increases are credited.
	Decreases are credited.	Decreases are debited.

7. A trial balance is a list of each account contained in the general ledger of an entity, together with its individual debit or credit balance. It is prepared in order to establish the equality of debits with credits before the preparation of the financial statements

8. A trial balance is used to prepare the financial statements. It shows the totals of each revenue and expense account that will appear on the income statement and the asset, liability, and equity balances that will appear on the balance sheet.

9. A general journal is a chronological record of an entity's financial transactions. It is often called a book of original entry because each transaction is recorded in the general journal first before it is posted to the entity's accounts.

10. The positioning of a debit-credit entry in the journal is similar in some respects to programming methods. In the following entry,

General Journal					
Date	Account/Explanation	PR	Debit	Credit
Dec. 1	Accounts Receivable		XX	
	Sales			XXX
	To record a sale on account.			

The positions represent the instructions "Post $XX to the debit side of the Accounts Receivable account" (thus increasing the accounts receivable) and "Post $XXX to the credit side of the Sales account" (thus increasing sales).

11. A general ledger is a book that contains the separate asset, liability, equity, revenue, and expense accounts of an entity. It is often referred to as a *book of final entry* and it is prepared so that the balance of each account can be found easily at any time.

12. A chart of accounts is a list of account names and numbers used in the general ledger, normally listed in the order of presentation on the financial statements. For example, accounts that appear on the balance sheet or on the income statement are grouped together. This facilitates the preparation of the financial statements.

13. The steps in the accounting cycle involve analyzing transactions, journalizing them in the general journal, posting from the general journal into the general ledger, preparing the trial balance, and generating financial statements are steps followed each accounting period. These steps form the core of the accounting cycle. Additional steps involved in the accounting cycle will be introduced in Chapter 3.

Chapter 3 Solutions

1. The sequence of financial transactions that occurs continuously during an accounting time period is called the *operating cycle*. Operations begin with some cash on hand. The cash is used to purchase supplies and pay expenses while revenue is being generated. When revenue is earned, cash is collected, beginning the cycle over again. While some transactions are being completed, others are only beginning.

2. No, the operating cycle does not have to be complete before income can be measured. Revenue can be recorded as earned when the product is sold or the service performed regardless of whether cash is collected. To measure income, expenses must be matched to revenues or the relevant time period. This usually can be done whether or not the operating cycle is complete.

3. Accrual accounting matches expenses to revenues for a particular time period. The accrual method is the basis on which accounts are adjusted to reach this objective. Under this method, expenses are matched to the revenues during the period that the revenues

are generated. The revenue recognition assumption helps determine when revenues are earned, thus allowing expenses to be matched to these revenues. Revenues are not generally matched to expenses by convention. The rationale is that revenues are recognised before expenses; therefore expenses should be matched to revenues.

4. Under the going concern concept, it is assumed that operating cycles that are incomplete at the end of financial periods will be completed during the (assumed) unlimited life of the entity. Since accountants must prepare financial statements even though operating cycles are incomplete, accrual accounting techniques are employed to more accurately measure economic activity during a given time period.

5.   a. The cost of goods that are transferred to customers (such as items sold); these expenses can be matched to revenue generated relatively easily.

   b. The cost of assets only partially consumed during the time period like trucks and equipment; these expenses are as easily matched with revenue.

   c. Some expenses incurred during the accounting period are not easily identified with revenue generated, such as salaries of administrative staff. These are matched to the period in which they are incurred, rather than to related revenue.

6. Adjusting entries are changes made at the end of an operating cycle to more accurately reflect economic activity during the period. For instance, depreciation is calculated on plant and equipment assets and charged to the income statement.

7. At the end of the accounting period, an accountant must determine the amount of future benefits (assets like Prepaid Insurance) that belong on the balance sheet and how much should be recorded in the income statement (as Insurance Expense, in this example). The appropriate amounts must be transferred by means of adjusting entries.

8. Plant and equipment accounts and are handled differently than other asset accounts. The expired portion of the cost of such an asset is estimated based on its useful life and recorded as depreciation expense. This requires no cash outlay, despite being an expense. Plant and equipment asset accounts themselves are not reduced by the depreciation expense; rather, a contra asset account is set up in order to show a reduced balance on the balance sheet.

9. A contra account is used to reduce the value of a related balance sheet item. For instance, the account Accumulated Depreciation-Equipment is credited by the amount of depreciation expense recorded each year. The balance in this account is netted against the related account (Equipment, in this example) so that the asset is shown at carrying amount on the balance sheet.

10. At the end of the accounting period, the amount of the liability that belongs on the balance sheet must be determined. The account balance is adjusted through the use of an adjusting entry to the related revenue account (Repair Revenue, in this example).

11. Accruals are assets and liabilities that increase during an accounting period but are not recognised in the normal course of recording financial transactions. They are recorded

through the use of accrual adjusting entries at the end of the accounting period. Examples of accounts that accrue are:

	Examples of Income Statement Account	Related Balance Sheet Account
Revenues:	Interest Earned	Interest Receivable
	Rent Earned	Unearned Rent
Revenue		
Expenses:	Interest Expense	Interest Payable
	Rent Expense	Prepaid Rent
	Insurance Expense	Prepaid Insurance
	Salaries Expense	Salaries Payable

Related balance sheet accounts are eventually reduced when cash is received or paid, as applicable.

12. An adjusted trial balance is prepared after posting the adjusting entries in order to establish the equality of debits and credits, and before preparing the financial statements.

13. The adjusted trial balance conveniently summarises the general ledger accounts in order of their appearance in the financial statements. This facilitates preparation of the financial statements.

14. The eight steps in the accounting cycle are:

   a. Transactions are analysed and recorded in the general journal.

   b. The journal entries are posted to general ledger accounts.

   c. An unadjusted trial balance is prepared to ensure debits equal credits.

   d. The account balances are analysed, and adjusting entries are prepared and posted.

   e. An adjusted trial balance is prepared to prove the equality of debits and credits.

   f. The adjusted trial balance is used to prepare financial statements.

   g. Closing entries are journalized and posted.

   h. A post-closing trial balance is prepared to ensure closing entries have been appropriately recorded and to ensure equality of debits and credits.

15. The first two steps in the accounting cycle occur continuously throughout the accounting period:

   a. Transactions are analysed and recorded in the general journal.

   b. The journal entries are posted to general ledger accounts.

16. The next six steps in the accounting cycle occur only at the end of the accounting period:

   a. An unadjusted trial balance is prepared to ensure debits equal credits.

   b. The account balances are analysed, and adjusting entries are prepared and posted.

   c. An adjusted trial balance is prepared to prove the equality of debits and credits.

   d. The adjusted trial balance is used to prepare financial statements.

   e. Closing entries are journalized and posted.

   f. A post-closing trial balance is prepared to ensure closing entries have been appropriately recorded and to ensure equality of debits and credits.

These steps differ from the others because they don't deal with individual transactions but address account balances. The adjusted balances are used to prepare financial statements.

17. Revenues must be accrued during the current accounting period if they have been earned and even if they have not yet been satisfied with cash during in the current accounting period. An account receivable is an example. Expenses must be accrued during the current accounting period if they relate to the revenue recognised during the current period or the current time period itself (for example, salaries) even if they have not yet been paid in cash. An account payable is an example. Cash outlays are recorded as prepaid expenses if cash is paid in advance of expense recognition. Prepaid Insurance is an example. For each such asset and liability, the accountant must determine at the end of the accounting period the appropriate balance that should be recorded on the balance sheet. These accounts are adjusted as appropriate through adjusting entries.

18. The need for regular financial information requires that revenue and expense accounts of a business be accumulated for usually no more than one year by convention, and that financial statements be prepared for that period. Using a consistent time period allows revenue and expenses for one period to be compared to a preceding period. A one-year cycle reduces effects of seasonal variations in business activity, for instance, but also allows for business performance to be evaluated by owners and creditors regularly and predictably.

19. Temporary accounts include all revenues and expense categories that are reduced to zero at the end of the fiscal year when they are closed to the Retained Earnings account. Permanent accounts have a continuing balance from one fiscal year to the next: these include all balance sheet accounts.

20. An income summary account is an account used only at year-end to accumulate all revenue and expense balances, and to reduce their general ledger accounts to zero at the end of the fiscal year. This account summarises the Net Income (or Net Loss) for the period. It is closed to the Retained Earnings account at year-end.

21. A post-closing trial balance is a listing of balance sheet accounts and their balances after all temporary accounts have been closed. It proves the equality of general ledger debit and credit balances before the next accounting period commences.

Chapter 4 Solutions

1. The economic resources of Big Dog Carworks Corp. are its assets: cash, accounts receivable, inventories, prepaid expenses and property, plant and equipment.

2. The financial statements are the balance sheet, the income statement, the statement of changes in equity, and the statement of cash flows. Notes to the financial statements are also included. The statements report the financial position of the company at year-end, the results of operations for the year, changes in share capital and retained earnings, sources and uses of cash during the year, and information in the notes that is not quantifiable or that provides additional supporting information to the financial statements.

3. Fundamentally, accounting measures the financial progress of an entity. The purpose of financial statements is to communicate information about this progress to external users, chiefly investors and creditors.

4. ASSETS = LIABILITIES + EQUITY

   $284,645 = 241,145 + 43,500.

5. Net assets equal $43,500 ($284,645 − 241,145). Net assets are synonymous with equity. They represent the amount of total assets attributable to the shareholders after taking into account the claims of creditors.

6. The individual assets of Big Dog Carworks Corp. as shown on the balance sheet are cash, accounts receivable, inventories, prepaid expenses, and property, plant, and equipment. Its liabilities are borrowings, accounts payable, and income taxes payable.

7. Per Note 3(d), property, plant, and equipment are depreciated on a straight-line basis over their estimated useful lives. Land is not depreciated.

8.   a. Current asset accounts: Per Note 3(a), revenue and expenses are accrued. This will give rise to current assets and current liabilities like accounts receivable, inventory, prepaid expenses, accounts payable, income taxes payable, and accrued liabilities. In addition, accounts receivable are carried at net realizable value. Per Note 3(e), inventory is carried at lower of cost and net realizable value. These amounts must be adjusted to the correct balance. Prepaid expenses would be adjusted to reflect the unused portion at the end of the period.

     b. Non-current asset accounts: Per Note 3(d), buildings are depreciated at 4% per year using the straight-line method. Equipment is depreciated at 10% per year on a straight-line basis; motor vehicles are depreciated on a straight-line basis over five years.

     c. Current liability accounts: income taxes payable are adjusted at the end of the period to reflect the estimated amount of taxes incurred for the period. All expenses that are incurred but not yet paid are added to the unrecorded accrual accounts. Examples are salaries payable for partial periods and interest owed but not yet paid.

d. Non-current liability accounts: borrowings must be analysed to determine current and non-current amounts, as shown in Note 5.

9. The balance sheet is classified in order to facilitate the analysis of its information. For instance, comparing amounts that will be needed to be satisfied within the upcoming year (current liabilities) with resources available to satisfy these claims (current assets) allows readers to assess the relative ability of the corporation to meets its short-term obligations as they become due.

10. Big Dog Carworks Corp. makes it easier to compare financial information from period to period by presenting comparative annual financial data for two years.

11. The auditor is H. K. Walker, Chartered Professional Accountant. The audit report states that the financial statements of BDCC have been examined in accordance with generally accepted auditing standards. It also states that, in the auditor'cs opinion, the statements present fairly the financial position of BDCC and the results of its operations and changes in financial position for the year just ended. There are no concerns raised in the report.

12. The auditor's report indicates that GAAP have been consistently applied in BDCC's financial statements (see last sentence of the report).

13. Management's responsibilities for financial statements are to ensure that they are prepared in accordance with GAAP, in this case International Financial Reporting Standards.

Though the financial statements are produced under the direction of management, they belong to the shareholders. Shareholders are the owners of the company.

Chapter 5 Solutions

1. A business providing a service holds no inventory for resale. Thus, a business that sells goods must match the cost of the goods sold with the revenue the sales generate. The Income Statement will show this, as well as the Gross Profit (also known as Gross Margin)— the difference between Sales and Cost of Goods Sold. A service business Income Statement would not show these items.

2. Gross Profit is the result of deducting Cost of Goods Sold from Sales (or Net Sales). For example, if a car is sold for $16,000 but cost $12,000, the Gross Profit calculation would be

Sales	$16,000
Cost of Goods Sold	12,000
Gross Profit	4,000

The profit on the sale, before considering operating and other expenses, is $4,000. The Gross Profit percentage is $4,000/16,000 or 25 per cent. That means for every $1 of Sales, the business earns $0.25 on average to cover operating and other expenses.

3. The Merchandise Inventory account collects information regarding the purchase of inventory, return to supplier of inventory, purchase discounts, transportation costs, and inventory shrinkage adjustments.

4. The sales and collection cycle starts off when a sale is made, often creating an Account Receivable. The Account Receivable is subsequently removed when cash is collected. If merchandise is returned because it is say, the wrong model or defective, a Sales Returns and Allowances records this amount and the Account Receivable is reduced. To speed up collections, discounts may be offered in return for prompt payments. If so, a Sales Discount may be given.

   Assuming a perpetual inventory system, the purchase and payment cycle starts with the purchase of merchandise, which becomes the inventory held for resale; the purchase generally creates an Account Payable. The Account Payable is removed once the account is paid by a cash disbursement. Purchases may be returned if the inventory item is wrong or defective. If so, the Account Payable would be reduced and a credit to Merchandise Inventory would be recorded. Discounts may be offered by the supplier to speed up payment by the purchaser. If so, the purchaser would be given a purchase discount which is debited to Account Payable and credited to Merchandise Inventory.

5. The contra accounts used for sales are

   a. Sales Returns and Allowances, which accumulates merchandise returned to the seller by the customer because of some defect or error.

   b. Sales Discounts, which accumulates discounts taken by customers when payments are made to the seller within the discount period.

   In a perpetual inventory system, there are no contra accounts used for purchases.

6. (Appendix) In a perpetual inventory system, the balances in Merchandise Inventory and Cost of Goods Sold are updated with each transaction involving purchases and sales. In a periodic inventory system, the balances in Merchandise Inventory and Cost of Goods Sold are not known until an inventory count is performed. The advantage of a perpetual system is that account balances are maintained in real time and therefore always known which is not the case for a periodic system where account balances have to be estimated until an inventory count is performed.

Chapter 6 Solutions

1. a. The amount of inventory on hand is important to management for two reasons. First, management wants to ensure there is ample inventory to meet all customers' orders. Second, because the cost of carrying inventory (for instance, rental of warehouse space, insurance) can be quite high, management wants to keep the inventory as low as possible.

b. Investors and creditors are concerned with the inventory because inventory is a large asset. They will want to assess its current amount and trends compared to other years and competitors' levels to help determine the financial strength of the company before investing or lending money, or for use as collateral, for instance.

2. Accountants must ensure the inventory is not obsolete or unsalable and that it is properly counted and valued, using an acceptable inventory cost flow assumption that is applied consistently from year to year.

3. The laid-down cost of inventory is the invoice price of the goods less purchase discounts, plus transportation-in, insurance while in transit, and any other expenditure made by the purchaser to get the merchandise to the place of business and ready for sale.

4. Flow of goods is the physical movement of the goods themselves as they enter the firm and are sold, especially when dealing with similar items, while the flow of costs is the costs assigned to the flow of goods in the firm using specific identification, FIFO, or average cost bases.

   GAAP does not require that the flow of costs basis be similar to the physical flow of goods, except when individual units of inventory can be identified by, for example, serial numbers. However, it does require that once the cost basis is selected, that it be followed consistently from period to period.

5. Two factors are considered in costing inventory: the quantity and the assigned value per unit. Assigning the value is often the more difficult aspect, as this involves tracking the laid-down costs of many items. Physical quantities can be tracked by computerised accounting systems and verified or determined by physical count at year-end.

6. Consistency in inventory costing is necessary for comparing a company's performance from year to year. GAAP does allow a company to change its inventory valuation method; however, the company must restate inventory and cost of goods sold effects on prior years using the new method. In practise this change is rarely made.

7. If the ending inventory is overstated at the end of 2018, then cost of goods sold is understated; therefore, the 2018 net income is overstated by $5,000. In 2019, the opening inventory would be overstated and cost of goods sold would be overstated; therefore, the net income would be understated by $5,000.

8. Inventory should be valued at less than cost when the lower of cost and net realisable value (LCNRV) principle is applied, perhaps due to factors such as physical deterioration, obsolescence, or changes in price levels.

9. The primary reason for the use of the LCNRV method of inventory valuation is to prevent overstatement. If the likely value of inventory has declined below cost, it is prudent to recognize the loss immediately, rather than when the goods are eventually sold. Net realisable value is the expected selling cost of inventory, less any applicable costs related to the sale.

10. When inventory is valued at LCNRV, cost refers to the laid-down cost.

11. The inventory cost flow assumptions permissible under GAAP are specific identification, FIFO or average cost.

12. Estimating inventory is useful for two reasons:

    a. It is useful for inventory control. When a total inventory amount is calculated under a periodic inventory system through physical count and valuation, an estimate can help check the accuracy.

    b. It is useful for the preparation of interim financial statements. Under a periodic inventory system, inventory on hand at any point in time is not readily available. To take a physical count often would be costly and inconvenient. An estimate offers a way of determining a company's inventory at any point in time in a cost-effective manner.

13. Under the gross profit method, the percentage of profit remaining after accounting for cost of goods sold (the gross profit percentage) is assumed to remain the same from year to year. By applying the rate to sales, gross profit and then cost of goods sold can be estimated. Opening inventory and purchases will be known from the accounting records, so cost of goods available for sale can be determined. The difference between the cost of goods sold and cost of goods available for sale is the ending inventory amount.

    Under the retail inventory method, mark-up on goods purchases then sold is considered to be constant. Both cost and selling prices of goods acquired are then valued at retail by using the mark-up amount. From this, the ending inventory at retail is calculated. By applying the cost percentage (costs of goods available for sale divided by retail costs of goods available for sale) to the retail ending inventory, its value at cost can be calculated.

    i. Example – gross profit method:

Sales		$100
Cost of Goods Sold:		
Opening Inventory (from records)	80	
Purchases (from records)	70	
Cost of Goods Available for Sale	150	
Ending Inventory	(a)?	(b)?
Gross Profit		$(c)?

    If the gross profit percentage average is 25%, the following can be estimated:

    (c) Gross profit   = 25% of $100   = $25
    (b) Cost of goods sold   = $100 − $25 (c)   = $75
    (a) Ending inventory   = $150 − $75 (b)   = $75

    Ending inventory (a) would be $75.

    ii. Example – retail inventory method; assumed mark-up = 200%:

	At Retail	At Cost
Sales	$500	$500
Cost of Goods Sold:		
Opening Inventory (records)	$(b)	$80
Purchases (records)	(b)	300
Cost of Goods Available for Sale	(c)	380
Ending Inventory	(d)?	(e)?
Cost of Goods Sold	(a)?	(f)?
Gross Profit (same as Sales)	$-0-	(g)?

(a) Cost of Goods restated at retail to equal sales = $500

(b) Opening Inventory and Purchases re-stated at retail = $300 × 200% = $600; = 80 × 200% = 160

(c) Cost of Goods Available at retail = $600 (b) + 160 (b) = $760

(d) Ending Inventory at retail = $760 (c) − 500 (a)
    = Cost of Goods Available at retail = $260
       − Cost of Goods Sold at retail

(e) Inventory at cost = Inventory at retail/200% = $260 (c)/200% = $130

(f) Cost of Goods Sold at cost = $380 − 130(e) = $250

(e) Gross Profit at cost = $500 − $250(e) = $250

14. The gross profit method is particularly useful in cases where goods have been stolen or lost in a fire; in such cases it is not possible to determine the balance in the ending inventory by a physical count when the periodic inventory system is used.

15. The retail inventory method assumes an average inventory cost flow assumption because the cost percentage used to calculate ending inventory and cost of goods sold is based on a constant mark-up.

Chapter 7 Solutions

1. Internal control is the system, plan, or organization established to ensure, as far as practical, the orderly and efficient conduct of business. In part, it is used to ensure accurate record-keeping and the timely preparation of financial statements, safeguard the assets of the business, and promote efficiency.

2. A bank reconciliation is a comparison of the items shown on the bank statement with the entries made in the records of the entity. A reconciliation leads to the update of the accounting records and the correction of errors, if any. Thus, control over cash is enhanced.

3. Different reconciling items that may appear in a bank reconciliation are as follows:

Book Reconciling Items	*Bank Reconciling Items*
Book errors	Outstanding deposits
NSF cheques	Outstanding cheques
Bank charges	Bank errors

4. The steps in preparing a bank reconciliation are (for which there is no specific order):

   a. Cancelled cheques returned by the bank are compared with cheques recorded as cash disbursements (both outstanding cheques from previous months and cheques written in current month's cash disbursements). Any outstanding cheques must be deducted from the bank statement ending balance.

   b. Other disbursements made by the bank are examined. These could include NSF (not sufficient funds) cheques or bank service charges. These must be deducted from the companies Cash account balance in the general ledger.

   c. The deposits shown on the bank statement are compared with the amounts recorded in the company records.

   d. The prior month's bank reconciliation is reviewed for outstanding deposits at the current date.

   e. Errors in the bank statement and in the company's record must be entered on the reconciliation.

5. A cheque received from trade customers that has been deposited but cannot be cleared by the bank because the customer's own bank balance is less than the amount of the cheque is an NSF (Not Sufficient Funds) cheque.

6. A petty cash system reimburses petty cash for an amount equal to the amounts disbursed when the fund has been depleted.

7. When a petty cash fund is established, a regular cheque is written for the amount to be held in the petty cash fund. The general ledger account Petty Cash is debited and Cash is credited. The cheque is cashed and the funds are held by the petty cash fund custodian.

   When the balance of cash in the funds held by the custodian is low, a cheque is written to reimburse the fund for the amount of all receipts held. The cheque is recorded as a debit to the applicable expense accounts and a credit to the Cash account in the general ledger.

8. Allowance for doubtful accounts is a contra accounts receivable account showing the estimated amount that will not be collected. To set it up, bad debt expense is debited and the allowance is credited for the estimated amount. In this way, the bad debt expenses for the period are matched with revenues for that period.

9. The income statement method for calculating the estimated amount of doubtful accounts assumes that a certain percentage of sales made on account will become uncollectible. The percentage is applied to credit sales and is chosen on the basis of bad debt experience of previous years. The estimated bad debt expense is calculated independently of any current balance in the Allowance for Doubtful Accounts general ledger account.

10. Ageing of accounts receivable is the detailed analysis of trade accounts receivable based on time that has elapsed since the creation of the receivable. An estimated loss percentage is applied to each time category to estimate an uncollectible amount. The estimated bad debt expense consists of the difference between the current balance in the Allowance for Doubtful Accounts general ledger account and the amount required to be set up based on this analysis.

11. The usual balance in the Accounts Receivable general ledger account is a debit. Occasionally, as a result of double payments, merchandise returns, or allowances granted for example, a credit balance occurs in some accounts. Theoretically, the credit balance should be transferred to liabilities. In practice, the net amount of accounts receivable is reported on the balance sheet unless the credits would materially distort the numbers reported.

Chapter 8 Solutions

1. To capitalize a cost means to record an expenditure as an asset instead of an expense.

2. An expenditure is a cash disbursement. A capital expenditure is one that

   a. Benefits more than the current accounting period, and these benefits are reasonably assured;

   b. Is material in amount.

   A revenue expenditure is an expense and does not have the characteristics belonging to a capital expenditure. NOTE: An expense is known as a revenue expenditure because its purpose is to generate revenue in the period in which it was expended (i.e., the current accounting period).

3. The purchase of a computer for business use qualifies as a capital expenditure when it benefits more than one accounting period. However, its purchase price may not be immaterial, depending on the company's capitalization policy. The annual maintenance or repairs made to the computer to keep it running are revenue expenditures if the cash disbursements are frequent, small, and do not extend the life of the computer. Purchase of a part that significantly enhances performance or extends the useful life of the computer might be capitalized, again depending on materiality.

4. Purchasing land and buildings for a lump sum means that no distinction is made between the two items at the time the purchase price is negotiated. The purchase price must be apportioned between the Land and Building accounts because buildings are subject to depreciation. The purchase price, therefore, is allocated on the basis of relative fair values of the land and the buildings.

5. As a matter of expediency, large companies set a dollar limit to help determine whether a disbursement is to be treated as a revenue or a capital expenditure because efforts required to capitalize and amortize an inexpensive item are so much greater than the benefits to be

derived. The concept of materiality is used to determine the amount at which an expenditure is considered capital in nature.

6. The three criteria are life of the part (whether it will benefit more than the current accounting period), the effect of the expenditure (whether it will enhance the service potential of the asset), and whether it is a material amount.

7. When one asset is exchanged for another, the cost of the asset acquired is determined by the fair value of the asset given up. If the fair value of the asset given up is not known, then the fair value of the asset acquired becomes the cost of the new asset.

8. Depreciation is the process of allocating the cost of a tangible, long-lived asset to each accounting period that will benefit from its use. The amount to be allocated is based on an estimate of the asset's useful life, residual value, and method of depreciation to be used.

9. As time elapses, the economic benefits provided by an asset may decrease, so that the efficiency of the asset is greater during its initial years and less later on. If a car is free from initial defect, it should not require any repairs in its first year of use, but it will need regular maintenance (e.g., oil changes). Eventually, it will likely require repairs, such as a replacement battery or new valves. The annual maintenance costs will increase, costing the user more to use the car. Therefore, the value of the car or the value of its services each year will decrease, so depreciation should be lower in subsequent years.

10. A usage method of depreciation is useful when the use of an asset varies from period to period and when wear and tear is the major cause of depreciation. A time-based method, such as straight-line depreciation, assumes that each period receives services of equal value from the use of the asset; time-based methods ignore asset usage. The preferable method is a matter of judgement.

    The sports car may wear out in two ways. The distance travelled has a large bearing on the value of the car; however, the passage of time also does, as an older model generally sells for less than its original cost. In terms of the useful life of the car, it will only last for a certain number of kilometres and it only renders services if it is driven. A usage method is likely best to measure depreciation, since the car is not necessarily driven for equal times during each period; the less it is driven, the more periods it will last.

11. Under the declining balance method, the calculation of depreciation is made without an adjustment for residual value. The asset cannot be depreciated below a reasonable residual value. The arithmetic of this formula is such that it will never reduce the asset balance to zero. Under the straight-line method, there is an adjustment made for residual value. This difference is not inconsistent, since both methods eventually result in a balance considered to be the residual value.

12. Under the declining balance method, a constant depreciation rate is applied in each accounting period to the remaining carrying amount (cost less accumulated depreciation). Both the depreciation expense and the carrying amount decline every period. Therefore, it is called the declining balance method.

Under the straight-line method, the depreciation expense for each accounting period is the same over the useful life of the asset.

13. If an asset is expected to have a 10-year life, then, each year 10 per cent of its life is over (100%/10 years = 10%). The double-declining balance is double this rate or 20% per year, calculated on the carrying amount of the asset at the end of the previous year.

14. Partial-year depreciation can be calculated using the half-year rule or by pro-rating depreciation expense over the number of months (rounded) that the asset was in use.

15. Either changes in estimated residual value or useful life may affect the calculation of depreciation expense. In both cases, no change is made to depreciation expense already recorded. The effects of the changes are spread over the remaining future periods.

16. Subsequent capital expenditures affect depreciation calculations in the same manner as changes in accounting estimates. The effects are accounted for prospectively (over the remaining future periods).

17. At the end of each reporting period, the recoverable amount (fair value less estimated costs of disposal) of an asset must be compared to its carrying value. If the recoverable amount is lower, the carrying value must be adjusted downward (a credit to the asset account) and an impairment loss must be recorded (a debit to an expense account). Subsequent years' depreciation expense calculations must also be adjusted.

18. Estimates of future events are commonplace in accounting, and necessary to provide more meaningful information to financial statement users, within reason. Depreciation is one example. The benefits of matching the use of a capital asset to the revenue of future periods which it helps to produce is deemed to be useful information under GAAP. To facilitate this, depreciation methods rely on estimates, and estimates of future events are subject to error. Accounting is intended to produce financial information that are not precise but rather that present a fair representation of the entity. If the estimates used subsequently prove to be incorrect, accountants change them.

19. Significant parts may have different estimated usage patterns, useful lives, and residual values. They may be replaced at different points in the useful life of the long-lived asset. Separate accounting for significant parts allows for these differences to be reflected in the financial statements.

20. A gain or loss on disposal does not occur when the carrying amount of an asset is the same as the proceeds of disposition.

21. A trade-in involves acquiring a long-lived asset by giving up a similar asset to the one being acquired (i.e., exchanging it) as part of the purchase price. It is not quite the same as an outright sale, which involves giving up a long-lived asset and receiving just cash for it.

22. The trade-in allowance may be higher or lower than the fair value of the used asset on the open market. Dealers often give more trade-in allowance on a used car than it is actually worth to make purchasers think that they are getting a better deal on the new car.

23. The cost of the new asset is calculated as the sum of cash paid plus the fair value of the trade-in.

24. Intangible assets, unlike property, plant, and equipment, cannot be touched or otherwise sensed. They are the same as PPE in that they represent future economic benefits to an entity over more than one accounting period, and so are similarly capitalized.

25. A patent is an exclusive right granted by the state to an inventor to produce and sell an invention for a specified period of time. A patent's useful life may be affected by economic factors based on demand and competition. The 20-year life may be excessive; a shorter life may be more realistic. For example, if a company develops a unique computer and patents it, even though it cannot be reproduced by other firms for 20 years, nothing stops a competitor from studying it, improving it, and patenting this improved computer. Although the "unique" computer may be useful for many years, it may be technologically obsolete before the patent expires.

26. A copyright is the exclusive right granted by the state to publish a literary or artistic work. It exists for the lifetime of the author and for a specific period of time after death. Similarly, a trademark is a legal right granted by the state, in this case for an entity to use a symbol or a word as a trademark to identify one of its products or services. A copyright would be granted for a piece of music or a novel. Examples of trademarks are the word "Coke"®on soft drink bottles and the stylised 'M'®of the McDonald's®logo.

27. Goodwill is a long-lived asset that represents the capitalized value of superior earnings potential of an acquired company. Goodwill is an asset but it is not an intangible asset. Such factors as favourable customer relations, loyal and competent employees, possession of valuable patents or copyrights, high-quality products, or effective management help create goodwill. Goodwill cannot be identified separately because it relates to the total entity acquired. Its useful life is considered indefinite unless its value is impaired because these attributes are assumed to continue into the future. Goodwill can only be purchased in an arms-length transaction because it is otherwise difficult to attach a value to it.

28. Intangible assets are generally measured and recorded at cost. The measurement basis should be disclosed, along with

   - the type of amortization method for each class of intangible asset;
   - opening and ending balances for cost, accumulated amortization, and carrying value, and disclosure of any changes;
   - whether they are internally generated; and
   - whether they have finite or indefinite lives.

Chapter 9 Solutions

1. A current liability is a form of debt that is expected to be paid within the longer of one year of the balance sheet date or one operating cycle. A long-term liability is also a form of debt but

it is expected to be paid beyond one year of the balance sheet date or the next operating cycle, whichever is longer. Current and long-term liabilities must be shown separately on the balance sheet.

2. Examples of known current liabilities are accounts payable, sales taxes payable, short-term notes payable, and payroll liabilities.

3. Known current liabilities are those where the payee, amount, and timing of payment are known. These are different from estimated current liabilities where the amount is not known and must be estimated.

4. Examples of estimated current liabilities include warranties and income taxes.

5. Estimated current liabilities are those where the amount is not known and must be estimated. The amount of an estimated current liability is probable and can be reliably estimated. A contingent liability is either not probably or it cannot be reliably estimated. Contingent liabilities are not recorded whereas estimated current liabilities are recorded.

6. A bond is a debt security that necessitates periodic interest payments during its life as well as a future repayment of the borrowed amount. A bond indenture is the contract that binds the corporation to the bondholders; it specifies the terms with which the corporation must comply and may restrict further borrowing by the corporation. A trustee may be used to serve as an impartial intermediary between the corporation and the bondholders, and so better balance the rights and needs of these two groups.

7. A bondholder has the following rights:

   a. The right to receive the face value of the bond at a specified maturity date in the future, that is, the right to receive the amount of money that was invested;

   b. The right to receive periodic interest payments at a specified per cent of the bond's face value; this interest represents the bondholder's return on investment; and

   c. The right to have the corporation pledge some secured assets to protect the bondholder's investment; this safeguard restricts excess borrowing and, in the event that interest or the face amount of the bonds cannot be paid, allows for the sale of these assets to generate the funds necessary for repayment.

8. Bond issues with different characteristics are disclosed separately in the financial statements, or more usually, in a note. The interest rate, maturity date, and any restrictions imposed on the corporation in the bond indenture, together with any assets pledged, also must be disclosed.

9. The different possibilities in the redemption of bonds before their maturity follow:

   a. The bonds can be repurchased on the open market if this option is financially advantageous to the issuer.

   b. The issuer may exercise a call provision if it is financially advantageous. A call provision, sometimes included in a bond indenture, permits early redemption at a specified price, usually higher than the face value.

c. The bondholder or issuer may exercise a conversion feature if provided for in the bond indenture, whereby the bonds can be converted into corporate shares.

10. If the bond contract interest rate is the same as the prevailing market interest rate, the bond will sell "at par". If the bond contract interest rate is higher than the prevailing market interest rate, the bond will sell at a premium. Prospective bondholders will bid up the price of the bonds because the bonds pay a rate of interest higher than other securities with similar features and risks. This creates a premium over the face value of the bonds. If the bond contract interest rate is lower than the prevailing market interest rate, the bond will sell at a discount because prospective bondholders will not be willing to pay the face value of the bonds. The issuer will have to accept a lower price so the effective interest rate will equal that of other securities with similar features and risks.

11. Under GAAP, an unamortised premium (discount) is added to (deducted from) the face value of the bond so that the liability is recorded at its carrying amount on the balance sheet.

12. If the bond contract interest rate is greater than that required in the market, then the bonds are sold at a premium. If the investment market operates efficiently, investor should earn only the market rate of interest. By paying a premium over the face value, the overall return to the investor is reduced from the bond contract rate to the market rate in effect at the issue date.

13. The *effective interest method* of amortisation calculates different amounts of amortisation from one period to another.

14. A loan, like a bond issue, is a means for an entity to raise investment capital through creditors. Both can be secured, and generally have fixed rates of interest and specified terms of repayment. However, loans are repaid with blended payments of interest and principal over the life of the liability. While the total payment on a loan is constant, the relative portion of interest decreases with each payment because loan principal is being reduced with each preceding payment. The portion of principal repayment increases. Bonds pay interest only to investors at regular intervals over the life of the issue plus a payment for the face value of the bond when it matures.

15. If money is borrowed today for one year, at the end of that year the money to be repaid is increased by the amount of interest charged. The future value is therefore the principal plus interest. If a certain sum must be repaid in one year, the value in today's money would exclude the interest to be earned in the future. This is its present value. The time value of money is represented by interest. Interest is added to the principal to obtain the future value, and it is removed from a future sum to arrive at the present value.

16. The price of a bond is determined by combining the present value of the following future cash flows associated with the bond:

a. a single amount, the face value, to be paid at maturity; and

b. semi-annual interest payments made during the bond's life.

Chapter 10 Solutions

1. The corporate form of organization offers the following advantages:

   a. It is a legal entity with unlimited life; its existence is separate from its owners; and it has many of the rights and responsibilities of an individual.

   b. It has limited liability; the owners are liable only for the amount they invest in the corporation.

   c. Acquiring capital is facilitated by being able to issue shares (ownership units) with different risk and reward structures to many owners.

   d. Corporations may pay income taxes at rates that may be lower than rates for individuals.

2. The owners of the corporation are liable for only the amount they have each invested. If the corporation fails, its assets are used to pay the creditors. If assets are not sufficient to pay all creditors, the shareholders have no further liability. Creditors are protected to some degree by disclosure of the corporation's limited liability.

3. Some of the rights of common shareholders are as follows:

   a. The right to participate in the management of the corporation by voting at shareholders' meetings (1 share generally equals 1 vote).

   b. The right to participate in dividends when they are declared by the corporation's board of directors.

   c. The right to participate in a distribution of assets on liquidation.

   d. The right to appoint auditors.

      The rights may be printed on the share certificate itself; they are detailed in the articles of incorporation.

4. The shareholders elect a board of directors, which appoints the officers of the corporation. The officers execute the policies approved by the board of directors. The directors are not involved in the daily management of the corporation.

5.   a. The two main classes of shares are:

      i. Preferred Shares – a class of shares that has a preference over common shares. Holders of preferred shares are entitled to payment of dividends before common shareholders and usually have prior claims on a corporation's assets on liquidation. A fixed dividend rate may be attached to the shares. Some preferred shares may have voting privileges.

      ii. Common Shares – the class of shares that are the basic ownership units in a corporation. Ownership of common shares carries the right to vote, to share in dividends, and to share in the assets of the corporation if it is liquidated; however, all other claims to the assets of a corporation rank ahead of the common shareholders' claims.

  b. Terms relating to the present status of a corporation's shares:

     i. Authorized Shares – the designated number of shares within each class of shares that a corporation may issue.

     ii. Unissued Shares – the shares of share capital in each class that a corporation is authorized to issue but has not yet issued.

     iii. Issued Shares – the total number of authorized shares that have been issued in the name of shareholders; issued shares may not actually be in the hands of shareholders (e.g., treasury shares).

     iv. Outstanding Shares – authorized shares that have been issued and are actually in the hands of shareholders.

     v. Reacquired Shares – shares that have been re-purchased from shareholders, have not been cancelled, and have not been reissued (also called treasury shares).

6. Shares are preferred in that their owners

  a. Generally assume less risk than common shareholders. When a corporation is dissolved, preferred shareholders have first claim on the remaining assets after the creditors have been paid; and

  b. Have a prior claim to the earnings of the corporation. Preferred shareholders must be paid specified dividends before any payments are made to common shareholders.

Preferred shareholders are similar to common shareholders in that both

  a. Own share certificates, evidence of corporate ownership;

  b. Have the legal guarantee that all shares of the same class will be treated equally with respect to rights and privileges attached to them;

  c. Have the right to dividends declared by the board of directors; and

  d. Have the right to participate in distribution of assets on liquidation of the corporation.

Preferred shareholders differ from common shareholders in that

  a. Common shareholders can participate in the management of the corporation by voting at shareholders' meetings (though some preferred shares may have voting privileges);

  b. Common shareholders can appoint auditors;

  c. Common shareholders assume more risk than preferred shareholders. However, common shareholders have more potential for receiving substantial dividends and increases in the value of their shares if the corporation is successful; and

  d. Common shareholders receive the balance of assets after other claims have been satisfied—in the case of a bankruptcy or liquidation, there are usually few or no other assets to distribute to common shareholders; preferred shareholders have prior claims.

7. When the shares of a corporation are selling at a high price on the stock market, management may opt for a share split in order to put them more easily within the reach of more investors.

8. The major components of the equity section of the balance sheet are share capital (preferred shares and common shares) and retained earnings. These two major components are distinguished because share capital represents invested capital not available for distribution to owners, while retained earnings are available for distribution as dividends.

9. Retained earnings represent net assets that are earned by a corporation over its life that have not been distributed as dividends to shareholders. As such, they can be used to invest in productive activities of the business.

10. Some of the main considerations involving the declaration of dividends are

   a. Whether or not there is enough cash, or whether the dividends can be paid by distribution of some other assets;

   b. Whether the policy of the corporation precludes dividend payments; and

   c. Whether there is a legal requirement that dividends must be declared.

11. A corporation may decide not to pay cash dividends even though it has a substantial net income because financial conditions may make it impractical or impossible.

   a. There may be insufficient cash, due to a significant investment in capital assets or reduction of debt, for instance. In a growth-oriented corporation, shareholders benefit from this strategy through increased earnings, which increase market prices for the shares.

   b. The policy of the corporation may preclude dividend payments.

   c. There is no legal requirement that dividends must be paid, unless otherwise specified by the various classes of shares.

   d. Dividends may be issued in shares of the corporation rather than in cash. A share dividend helps to preserve cash or to increase the number of shares traded on the stock market.

12. *The date of dividend declaration*: the corporation is legally required to pay the dividend; a liability is established.

   The date of record: shareholders who own the shares on this date will receive the dividend.

   The date of payment: the dividend is actually paid on this date.

13. A cash dividend reduces both the asset Cash and the equity account Retained Earnings. A share dividend does not affect Cash; the Retained Earnings account is still reduced, but the account Common Shares (or Preferred, if applicable) is increased. A share dividend has no net effect on equity.

14. Dividend preferences that may be attached to preferred shares are

   a. Preferred shareholders are entitled to dividends before any dividends are distributed to common shareholders;

b. Preferred shares may be cumulative; undeclared dividends can accumulate from one year to the next; and

c. Preferred shareholders may participate with common shareholders in dividend distributions beyond their usual preferred dividends.

Preferred shares have returns that are more predictable and thus attract investors with a lower tolerance for risk. These advantages do not mean that purchasing preferred shares are necessarily better than purchasing common shares. Holding common shares has its own advantages. Common shareholders generally have legal control of the corporation. Ownership of commons shares carries the right to vote, to earn potentially unlimited dividends, and to have share values increase on stock markets.

15. If preferred shares are cumulative, undeclared dividends from previous years are accumulated and must be paid along with the current dividend. The unpaid dividends are called dividends in arrears. They are not a liability of the corporation unless dividends have been declared by the board of directors.

16. A share dividend is a dividend in the form of shares of the corporation. Retained earnings decrease and share capital increases. A share split is an action taken by the corporation to increase the number of shares outstanding and reduce the per-share market value. No journal entry is required to record a share split, and there is no effect on the accounting records.

17. A share dividend increases the number of shares held by each shareholder but the ownership percentage remains the same. If a 10 per cent share dividend is distributed, each shareholder holds more shares but the percentage of ownership remains the same, illustrated as follows:

	Ownership				
	Before Share Dividend			*After Share Dividend*	
Shareholders	*Shares*	*%*		*Shares*	*%*
W	250	25%		275	25%
X	250	25%		275	25%
Y	250	25%		275	25%
Z	250	25%		275	25%
	1,000	100%		1,100	100%

Chapter 11 Solutions

1. A statement of cash flows (SCF) provides external readers of a corporation's financial statements with a summary of the cash transactions that took place in the company in a particular period. For example, a reader could determine the amount of proceeds from the sale of plant and equipment assets, or whether plant and equipment assets were acquired.

It communicates how the company is financing its activities (internally from operations or externally from other sources), and why cash increased or decreased.

Its advantage over the balance sheet is that the balance sheet reports the financial position of the company at a particular point in time, while the SCF reports the changes in cash that occurred from one balance sheet date to another.

An income statement reports earnings on an accrual basis, which is important. However, investors and creditors are also interested in determining how a corporation has generated and used cash during a fiscal period, because cash is an important determinant of liquidity. The SCF provides this information succinctly to readers.

2. These activities are important to readers who wish to evaluate the financial position and the results of operations of a particular company in order to make certain decisions, such as whether or not to invest in it. The extent of cash flows resulting from financing and investing decisions can help readers identify the underlying, longer-range activities of the firm that may affect future earnings, such as whether plant and equipment assets are being acquired, or debt is being retired. The SCF makes these activities explicit.

3. An increase in accounts receivable during a fiscal year is recorded by a debit. The offsetting credit to the Cash account denotes a use of cash. In effect, cash has been diminished because amounts owing by customers has increased, instead of being collected.

4. The declaration of cash dividends has no effect on cash flow, since it does not involve the use of cash; it merely sets up a dividend payable in the books of the company. The payment of a dividend declared decreases cash flow, since it involves the outlay of cash. Whether the dividend was declared in prior years or in the current year has no effect; only the payment reduces cash. Changes in the dividends payable account balance from one year to the next also affect cash flows. A net reduction in dividends payable (a debit) increases cash outflow (a credit). A net increase in dividends payable decreases cash outflow.

5. Buying or selling short-term investments may decrease or increase the amount of cash available to the company if they are considered part of cash and cash equivalents. If they are considered part of C&CE, transactions involving short-term investments have no effect on cash flow from operating activities.

6. Net income for a period usually consists of sales less cost of sales, operating expenses, and other expenses like interest and income taxes. If there are a large number of credit sales and the amount of accounts receivable over the last year has increased, then there is less cash inflow compared to sales revenue recorded on the income statement. If many expenses are prepaid, then cash has been used but the expenses have not decreased net income. Similarly, if inventory levels have increased from one year-end to the next, cash has decreased but cost of goods sold is unaffected on the income statement.

Depreciation of property, plant, and equipment decreases net income but not cash. Losses and gains on sale of property, plant, and equipment assets affect net income, but do not affect cash flows. Cash may also be used to purchase property, plant, and equipment, pay off borrowings, and pay dividends, as examples. These investing and financing activities affect cash, but are not reflected on the income statement.

7. Main balance sheet account transactions that use cash are (a) operations of the company (net cash outflow from operating activities during the period), (b) purchase of property, plant and equipment assets, (c) retirement of debt and share capital, and (d) payment of dividends. The balance sheet accounts are analysed by looking at the opening and ending balances of the account, determining the reasons for the change in the account, and recording the effects as a cash inflow or outflow from operating, financing, or investing activities.

Chapter 12 Solutions

1. Comparisons can be made using published industry statistics, statistics of previous years, statistics of leading competitors, or internally-developed ratios.

2. Liquidity is a corporation's ability to pay current liabilities as they become due. Being "illiquid" means creditors that have provided the corporation with goods and services on account, or with other forms of short-term borrowing, cannot be paid. Implications of being illiquid:

   Creditors:

   a. Can refuse to provide further goods or services on account.

   b. Can sue for payment.

   c. Can put the corporation into receivership or bankruptcy.

   d. Can refuse to lend additional cash.

   e. Can demand repayment of all debts, including long-term debt.

   Shareholders:

   a. May be unwilling to invest in additional share capital of the corporation

   b. Risk the loss of their investments if the company becomes bankrupt

3. Net income is based on accrual accounting and not cash basis accounting. For example, if $1,000,000 of sales are on account, this transaction increases net income but not cash. As an additional example, the corporation may have large sums of capital tied up in inventory which means there is less cash available to pay the liabilities.

4. *Current ratio*: Indicates how many current asset dollars exist to pay current liabilities.

   Acid-test ratio: Indicates whether or not the corporation is able to meet the immediate demands of creditors, without considering current assets tied up in inventory or prepaid expenses.

   Accounts receivable collection period: Indicates the average time needed to collect receivables.

   Number of days of sales in inventory: Indicates how many days of sales can be made with inventory on hand.

Revenue operating cycle: Indicates how long it is between the purchase of inventory and the subsequent collection of cash from sales of inventory.

5. **a.** Working capital is the difference between current assets and current liabilities.

    The current ratio is computed by dividing current assets by current liabilities. It is one measure of whether or not the corporation is able to repay short-term creditors. The acid-test ratio, on the other hand, is a more severe test of liquidity. It is computed by dividing quick assets (cash, short-term investments, accounts receivable) by current liabilities.

    b. The current ratio is only a rough indication of how able an entity is to pay its current liabilities as they become due. The relative liquidity of components of current assets is not considered in the calculation of this ratio. The acid-test ratio is often used as a more severe test of liquidity.

6. The ability to pay short-term creditors as amounts become due depends on the liquidity of the current assets. If, for example, company X's current assets consist of cash and company Y's current assets consist of inventory, company Y will not be able to pay its creditors easily because of a lack of cash.

7. Taking too long to collect accounts receivable will reduce the amount of cash available to pay liabilities as they become due. The same is true if there is an over-investment in inventory.

8. An acceptable number of days to collect accounts receivable and to convert inventory to sales depends on several factors, including the industry in which the corporation does business and the state of the economy. Management judgement and experience are crucial. If accounts receivable are collected too slowly, or if credit is extended to liberally, debts may not be collected in a timely manner, or at all. If accounts receivable collections are too short, potential credit sales may be lost. Similarly, higher number of days of sales in inventory indicates that more cash is tied up in inventory. On the other hand, a lower number of days of sales in inventory may indicate that inventory levels are too low. Potential sales may be lost.

9. Advantages of decreasing number of days of sales in inventory might be that

    a. The amount of assets tied up in inventory is reduced.

    b. The dangers of obsolescence or deterioration are reduced.

    c. Less storage space is used for inventory, so that warehousing expenses are reduced.

    A disadvantage of decreasing number of days of sales in inventory is that stock can be reduced to the point where sales are lost.

10. The revenue operating cycle indicates the number of days that elapse between the purchase of inventory and the subsequent collection of cash after a sale is made. It is computed by adding the average number of days needed to turn over inventory and the average number of days needed to collect receivables. It is useful in evaluating liquidity because a comparison can be made of the number of days needed to complete the cycle and the number of

days within which the payables are due. Management can determine how long it will take the corporation to pay reinvest in inventory with cash generated by the revenue operating cycle.

11.   **a.** Ratios that measure margins on sales:

   i. *Gross profit ratio*: indicates the amount of revenue left to cover other expenses after deducting cost of goods sold. It is calculated by dividing gross profit by net sales.

   ii. *Operating profit ratio*: indicates the amount of revenue left to cover interest and income taxes expenses after deducting cost of goods sold and operating expenses. It is calculated by dividing income from operations by net sales.

   iii. *Net profit ratio*: Indicates the percentage of sales revenue left in the business after payment of operating expenses, interest, and income taxes. It is calculated by dividing net income by net sales.

   b. Ratios that measure returns on balance sheet items:

   i. Sales to total assets ratio: Indicates the adequacy of sales in relation to average total assets. It is calculated by dividing net sales by average total assets. In the longer term, typically investments in property, plant and equipment assets make up the majority of assets that generate sales and so PPE is sometimes used as a good estimate when calculating this ratio.

   ii. Return on total assets ratio: Indicates how efficiently a company uses all of its balance sheet assets to earn income from operations. It is calculated by dividing income from operations by average total assets.

   iii. Return on equity ratio: Indicates the amount of income that is generated by shareholders' proportion of total assets. It is calculated by dividing net income by average equity.

12. Analysts and investors are concerned with the financial structure of a corporation because the higher the reliance on debt, the more substantial claim the creditors have against the assets of the corporation. The corporation is also more vulnerable to rises in interest rates and economic downturns, which in turn affects future earnings expectations.

13. Reliance on creditor financing can be positive, since financing a corporation by issuing additional shares results in a dilution of existing shareholders' control of the corporation. Also, creditor financing is beneficial to shareholders when the return is greater than the interest paid on the debt. However, interest has to be paid on the debt and, ultimately, the debt itself has to be repaid. Interest reduces the income of the corporation. If interest rates paid on debt are higher than the returns generated from the borrowed funds, net income is reduced. The corporation is more susceptible to economic downturns and interest rate increases as its reliance on debt grows.

14. *Short-Term Financing* Advantages:

   a. Usually does not require interest payment to the creditors

   b. Easily obtained

Disadvantages:

   a. Payment is required within a short time

   b. More risky, because it has to be renewed more frequently

Long-Term Financing Advantages:

   a. More secure, because renewal is infrequent

   b. Principal repayment not required for a long time

Disadvantages:

   a. Must pay interest, and legal documents are often signed to enforce this.

   b. More work to acquire (must present financial statements, may have to be audited)

15.   **a.** *Earnings per share*: Indicates the amount of net income that has been earned on each common share. It is calculated by dividing (net income less preferred share dividends) by number of common shares outstanding.

    b. *Price-earnings ratio*: Indicates the reasonableness of the market price in relation to per-share earnings. It is calculated by dividing market price per share by earnings per share.

    c. *Dividend yield*: Indicates the short-term cash return that could be expected from an investment in a company's shares. It is calculated by dividing dividends declared by outstanding common shares.

16. Horizontal analysis is the comparison of the change in one item on financial statements (such as merchandise inventory) during two or more accounting periods. Vertical analysis is the analysis of the composition of a financial statement by restating all items in that statement as percentages of a total. Generally sales is used as the income statement base and total assets (or total liabilities and equity) is used as the balance sheet base. Comparing the percentages of a particular item between two or more years shows the change in composition of the statement components.

Chapter 13 Solutions

1. A partnership is an unincorporated form of business organisation in which the entity is owned by two or more persons. Five characteristics of a partnership are:

   a. *Limited life* – if a partner is admitted, withdraws, or dies, the existing partnership is dissolved and the business continues under a new partnership agreement.

   b. *Unlimited liability* – in general, each partner is personally liable for the debts that the partnership cannot pay. In the event that a partner cannot pay his/her share of partnership debts, the other partners can be called on to pay personally for such debts.

c. *Mutual agency* – each partner can make binding agreements not only on the partnership, but also on the other partners.

d. *Co-ownership of assets* – all assets contributed to the partnership by individual partners are jointly owned by all partners.

e. *Sharing of profits and losses* – if the partnership agreement does not stipulate how profits and losses will be shared, all profits and losses are shared equally.

2. The advantages of a partnership are:

   a. The knowledge, skills, and financial resources of two or more persons can be combined.

   b. Partnerships can be formed relatively easily and quickly.

   c. A partnership can act promptly as a business enterprise in all matters. A corporation may be restricted in its actions on certain matters by its charter, by laws, or by statute.

   d. Many of the formal government reports required of a corporation are not required of the partnership.

   e. Income taxes are not levied against partnerships. The partners, however, report on their individual tax returns their share of partnership income.

   The disadvantages of partnerships are:

   a. Liability is usually unlimited. Partners are liable for all debts of the partnership.

   b. The life of the partnership is limited. Death, withdrawal, or admission of a partner; agreement to terminate; bankruptcy; and incapacity of a partner are all terminate a partnership.

   c. The partnership is a mutual agency; that is, each partner may act in business matters as the agent of the partnership.

   d. The ability of a partnership to raise funds may be limited.

3. Although a proprietorship, partnership, and corporation engage in the same equity transactions of investment, distribution of income, and incomes/losses, how they are recorded is different.

   In a proprietorship, there is only one equity account: owner's capital. Investments by the owner, distributions of income known as withdrawals, and incomes/losses are all recorded in the owner's capital account.

   In a partnership, there is a capital account for each partner. A partner's investments, distributions of income in the form of withdrawals, and a share of incomes/losses are all recorded in the partner's capital account.

   In a corporation, there are two types of equity accounts: share capital and retained earnings. Investments by the owners, known as shareholders, are recorded in share capital. Distributions of income, known as dividends, along with incomes/losses are recorded in retained earnings.

4. Profits and losses are divided equally among partners if no agreement exists. Otherwise, several methods may be followed to allocate profits or losses Formulas often consider three factors – a return to each partner based on relative levels of services rendered, a return on capital invested, and a further division of remaining profits and losses according to a fixed ratio.

5. Salary and interest allocations are included in the division of profits and losses because the time and effort contributed by individual partners to the business and the amount of contributed capital may differ among partners.

6. The balance sheet of a partnership merely shows the ending capital balance of each partner. If many partners exist, a total capital amount is shown and the details of each partner's capital account appear in a statement of changes in equity.

Chapter 1 Solutions

EXERCISE 1–1

   a. Partnership

   b. International Financial Reporting Standards

   c. Ethics

   d. Financial accounting

   e. Managerial accounting

   f. Separate legal entity

   g. Limited liability

   h. Unlimited liability

EXERCISE 1–2

   a. 30,000

   b. 9,000

   c. 95,000

   d. In **a**, debt financing $= (20,000/50,000) \times 100 = 40\%$. In **b**, debt financing $= (9,000/10,000) \times 100 = 90\%$. In **c**, debt financing $= (15,000/95,000) \times 100 = 15.79\%$ (rounded to two decimal places). Therefore, the greatest percentage of debt financing is reflected in **b**.

   e. In **a**, equity financing $= 100 - 40 = 60\%$. In **b**, equity financing $= 100 - 90 = 10\%$. In **c**, equity financing $= 100 - 15.79 = 84.21\%$. Therefore, the greatest percentage of equity financing is reflected in **c**.

EXERCISE 1–3

	ASSETS	=	LIABILITIES	+		EQUITY	
Cash	+ Equipment	=	Accounts Payable	+	Share Capital	+	Retained Earnings

A. Retained earnings $= \$5,000\ (3,000 + 8,000 - 4,000 - 2,000)$

B. Accounts payable $= \$3,000\ (1,000 + 6,000 - 3,000 - 1,000)$

C. Cash $= \$1,000\ (4,000 - 1,500 - 3,000 - 500)$

D. Retained earnings $= \$6,000\ (6,000 + 7,000 - 3,000 - 4,000)$

E. Equipment $= \$3,500\ (2,500 - 4,500 - 500 - 1,000)$

EXERCISE 1–4

a. ASSETS = LIABILITIES + EQUITY

Equity at Jan. 1 $= \$10,000\ (\$50,000 - 40,000)$

Equity at Dec. 31 $= \$20,000\ (\$40,000 - 20,000)$

The increase in equity during the year was $10,000 ($20,000 ending equity − 10,000 beginning equity). Given that during the year no share capital was issued and no dividends were declared, $10,000 is the amount of net income earned during 2015.

b. ASSETS = LIABILITIES + EQUITY

Equity at Jan. 1 $= \$10,000\ (\$50,000 - 40,000)$

Equity at Dec. 31 $= \$20,000\ (\$40,000 - 20,000)$

The increase in equity during the year was $10,000 ($20,000 ending equity − 10,000 beginning equity). Given that during the year no share capital was issued and $5,000 of dividends were declared, $15,000 is the amount of net income earned during 2015 [calculated as net income − $5,000 dividends = $10,000 increase in equity; net income = 10,000 + 5,000 or 15,000].

c. ASSETS = LIABILITIES + EQUITY

Equity at Jan. 1 $= \$10,000\ (\$50,000 - 40,000)$

Equity at Dec. 31 $= \$20,000\ (\$40,000 - 20,000)$

The increase in equity during the year was $10,000 ($20,000 ending equity − 10,000 beginning equity). Given that during the year $12,000 of share capital was issued and no dividends were declared, a net loss of $2,000 was realized for 2015 (calculated as net income + $12,000 share capital issued = $10,000 increase in equity; net income = $10,000 − $12,000; net income is therefore a negative $2,000 which represents a net loss).

d. ASSETS = LIABILITIES + EQUITY

Equity at Jan. 1 $= \$10,000\ (\$50,000 - 40,000)$

Equity at Dec. 31 = $20,000 ($40,000 − 20,000)

The increase in equity during the year was $10,000 ($20,000 ending equity − 10,000 beginning equity). Given that during the year $8,000 of share capital was issued and $12,000 of dividends were declared, $14,000 is the amount of net income earned during 2015 (calculated as net income + $8,000 share capital issued − $12,000 dividends = $10,000 increase in equity; net income = $10,000 − $8,000 + $12,000; net income = $14,000).

EXERCISE 1–5

a.	L	h.	A	o.	L
b.	A	i.	A	p.	E
c.	L	j.	E	q.	A
d.	A	k.	E	r.	E
e.	A	l.	A	s.	E
f.	E	m.	E	t.	A
g.	L	n.	E		

EXERCISE 1–6

1. ASSETS   = Cash + Accounts Receivable + Unused Supplies + Land + Building + Equipment
   = $33,000 + $82,000 + $2,000 + $25,000 + $70,000 + $30,000
   = $242,000 Total Assets

2. LIABILITIES = Bank Loan + Accounts Payable
   = $15,000 + $27,000
   = $42,000 Total Liabilities

3. ASSETS   = LIABILITIES + EQUITY
   EQUITY   = $242,000 Total Assets − $42,000 Total Liabilities
   = $200,000 Total Equity

Since equity is $200,000 and retained earnings is $40,000, share capital must be $160,000.

EXERCISE 1–7

EDW Inc.
Income Statement
Month Ended March 31, 2015

Revenues		
Service Revenue		$20,000
Expenses		
Wages Expense	$9,000	
Miscellaneous Expense	2,500	
Insurance Expense	1,500	
Office Supplies Expense	1,000	14,000
Net Income		$6,000

EDW Inc.
Statement of Changes in Equity
Month Ended March 31, 2015

	Share Capital	Retained Earnings	Total Equity
Opening Balance	$ -0-	$ -0-	$ -0-
Shares Issued	2,000		2,000
Net Income		6,000	6,000
Ending Balance	$2,000	$6,000	$8,000

EDW Inc.
Balance Sheet
March 31, 2015

Assets		Liabilities	
Cash	$1,000	Accounts Payable	$5,000
Accounts Receivable	4,000		
Equipment	8,000		
		Equity	
		Share Capital	$2,000
		Retained Earnings	6,000
		Total Equity	8,000
Total Assets	$13,000	Total Liabilities and Equity	$13,000

NOTE:

The $2,000 amount for shares issued was calculated using $A = L + E$ or, using the accounts in the order given in the alphabetized information; $4,000 + 1,000 + 8,000 = 5,000 - 1,500 - 2,500 - 1,000 + 20,000 + Share\ Capital - 9,000$; $13,000 = 11,000 + Share\ Capital$; $13,000 - 11,000 = 2,000\ Share\ Capital$.

Alternatively, you could have inserted all the values from the alphabetized information into the financial statements and then solved for the unknown Share Capital amount. There is often more than one approach to solving math related questions.

EXERCISE 1–8

Algonquin Inc.
Income Statement
Year Ended July 31, 2015

Revenues		
Service Revenue		$81,000
Expenses		
Advertising Expense	$5,000	
Insurance Expense	7,000	
Salaries Expense	64,000	76,000
Net Income		$5,000

Algonquin Inc.
Statement of Changes in Equity
Year Ended July 31, 2015

	Share Capital	Retained Earnings	Total Equity
Opening Balance	$10,000	$6,000	$16,000
Net Income		5,000	5,000
Dividends		(2,000)	(2,000)
Ending Balance	$10,000	$9,000	$19,000

Algonquin Inc.
Balance Sheet
July 31, 2015

Assets		Liabilities		
Cash	$9,000	Accounts Payable	$3,000	
Accounts Receivable	17,000	Note Payable	18,000	
Machinery	14,000	Total Liabilities		$21,000
		Equity		
		Share Capital	$10,000	
		Retained Earnings	9,000	
		Total Equity		19,000
Total Assets	$40,000	Total Liabilities and Equity		$40,000

EXERCISE 1–9

Algonquin Inc.
Income Statement
Year Ended July 31, 2015

Revenues		
Service Revenue		$81,000
Expenses		
Advertising Expense	$5,000	
Insurance Expense	7,000	
Salaries Expense	64,000	76,000
Net Income		$5,000

Algonquin Inc.
Statement of Changes in Equity
Year Ended July 31, 2015

	Share Capital	Retained Earnings	Total Equity
Opening Balance	$7,000	$6,000	$13,000
Shares Issued	3,000		3,000
Net Income		5,000	5,000
Dividends		(2,000)	(2,000)
Ending Balance	$10,000	$9,000	$19,000

Algonquin Inc.
Balance Sheet
July 31, 2015

Assets		Liabilities		
Cash	$9,000	Accounts Payable	$3,000	
Accounts Receivable	17,000	Note Payable	18,000	
Machinery	14,000	Total Liabilities		$21,000
		Equity		
		Share Capital	$10,000	
		Retained Earnings	9,000	
		Total Equity		19,000
Total Assets	$40,000	Total Liabilities and Equity		$40,000

NOTE:

Given that additional shares were issued for cash of $3,000 during the year ended July 31, 2015 and share capital had a balance of $10,000 at July 31, 2015, the end of the year, the beginning balance in share capital must have been $7,000.

EXERCISE 1–10

Wallaby Inc.
Income Statement
Month Ended March 31, 2015

Revenues		
Fees Earned		$12,000
Expenses		
Equipment Rental Expense	$9,400	
Wages Expense	3,400	
Fuel Expense	500	13,300
Net Loss		$1,300

Wallaby Inc.
Statement of Changes in Equity
Month Ended March 31, 2015

	Share Capital	Retained Earnings	Total Equity
Opening Balance	$6,400	$4,000	$10,400
Net Loss		(1,300)	(1,300)
Ending Balance	$6,400	$2,700	$9,100

Wallaby Inc.
Balance Sheet
March 31, 2015

Assets			Liabilities		
Cash	$6,000		Rent Payable	$2,500	
Accounts Receivable	1,600		Note Payable	18,000	
Truck	22,000		Total Liabilities		$20,500
			Equity		
			Share Capital	$6,400	
			Retained Earnings	2,700	
			Total Equity		9,100
Total Assets	$29,600		Total Liabilities and Equity		$29,600

EXERCISE 1–11

Adams Ltd.
Income Statement
For the Month Ended January 31, 2015

Revenue		
Service Revenue		$3,335
Expenses		
Rent expense	$300	
Repairs expense	500	
Salaries expense	1,000	
Miscellaneous expense	335	
Total expenses		2,135
Net Income		$1,200

Adams Ltd.
Statement of Changes in Equity
For the Month Ended January 31, 2015

	Share Capital	Retained Earnings	Total Equity
Opening balance	$ -0-	$ -0-	$ -0-
Shares issued	3,000	-0-	3,000
Net income	-0-	1,200	1,200
Ending balance	$3,000	$1,200	$4,200

Adams Ltd.
Balance Sheet
At January 31, 2015

Assets

Cash	$1,000	
Land	1,000	
Building	2,500	
Total assets		$4,500

Liabilities

Accounts payable		$300

Equity

Share capital	$3,000	
Retained earnings	1,200	
Total equity		4,200
Total liabilities and equity		$4,500

EXERCISE 1–12

a.

	Assets	=	Liabilities	+	Equity	
Balances at April 1, 2015	$100,000		$60,000		$40,000	
					10,000	April net income(loss)
Balances at April 30, 2015	$180,000	=	$130,000	+	$50,000	

b.

	Assets	=	Liabilities	+	Equity	
Balances at April 1, 2015	$100,000		$60,000		$40,000	
					$50,000	Shares issued in April
					(40,000)	April net income(loss)
Balances at April 30, 2015	$180,000	=	$130,000	+	$50,000	

c.

	Assets	=	Liabilities	+	Equity	
Balances at April 1, 2015	$100,000		$60,000		$40,000	
					14,000	April net income(loss)
					(4,000)	Dividends paid in April
Balances at April 30, 2015	$180,000	=	$130,000	+	$50,000	

EXERCISE 1–13

a.

	Assets	=	Liabilities	+	Equity	
Balances at June 1, 2015	$160,000		$100,000		$60,000	
					$70,000	June net income(loss)
					(20,000)	Dividends paid in June
Balances at June 30, 2015	$200,000	=	$90,000	+	$110,000	

b.

	Assets	=	Liabilities	+	Equity	
Balances at June 1, 2015	$160,000		$100,000		$60,000	
					$40,000	Shares issued in June
					$90,000	June net income(loss)
					(80,000)	Dividends paid in June
Balances at June 30, 2015	$200,000	=	$90,000	+	$110,000	

c.

	Assets	=	Liabilities	+	Equity	
Balances at June 1, 2015	$160,000		$100,000		$60,000	
					$130,000	Shares issued in June
					($80,000)	June net income(loss)
					-0-	Dividends paid in June
Balances at June 30, 2015	$200,000	=	$90,000	+	$110,000	

EXERCISE 1–14

a.	3	Purchased a truck for cash.
b.	1	Issued share capital for cash.
c.	2	Incurred a bank loan as payment for equipment.
d.	3	Made a deposit for electricity service to be provided to the company in the future.
e.	4	Paid rent expense.
f.	NT	Signed a new union contract that provides for increased wages in the future.
g.	NT	Wrote a letter of complaint to the prime minister about a mail strike and hired a messenger service to deliver letters.
h.	4	Received a collect telegram from the prime minister; paid the messenger.
i.	1	Billed customers for services performed.
j.	5	Made a cash payment to satisfy an outstanding obligation.
k.	3	Received a payment of cash in satisfaction of an amount owed by a customer.
l.	1	Collected cash from a customer for services rendered.
m.	4	Paid cash for truck operation expenses.
n.	5&4	Made a monthly payment on the bank loan; this payment included a payment on part of the loan and also an amount of interest expense. (Hint: This transaction affects more than two parts of the accounting equation.)
o.	7	Issued shares in the company to pay off a loan.

Chapter 2 Solutions

EXERCISE 2–1

	Assets		Liabilities		Equity	
	Debit	*Credit*	*Debit*	*Credit*	*Debit*	*Credit*
	(increase)	(decrease)	(decrease)	(increase)	(decrease)	(increase)
2. Borrowed $5,000 from the bank.	5,000			5,000		
3. Paid $2,000 of the bank loan.		2,000	2,000			
4. Paid $600 in advance for a one-year insurance policy.	600	600				
5. Received $500 in advance for next month's rental of office space.	500			500		

EXERCISE 2–2

	Debit	Credit
2. Purchased equipment on credit.	Equipment	Accounts Payable
3. Paid for a one-year insurance policy.	Prepaid Expenses	Cash
4. Billed a customer for repairs completed today.	Accounts Receivable	Repair Revenue
5. Paid this month's rent.	Rent Expense	Cash
6. Collected the amount billed in transaction 4 above.	Cash	Accounts Receivable
7. Collected cash for repairs completed today.	Cash	Repair Revenue
8. Paid for the equipment purchased in transaction 2 above.	Accounts Payable	Cash
9. Signed a union contract.	No Entry	No Entry
10. Collected cash for repairs to be made for customers next month.	Cash	Unearned Revenue
11. Transferred this month's portion of prepaid insurance that was used to Insurance Expense.	Insurance Expense	Prepaid Expenses

EXERCISE 2–3

Cash		Bank Loan		Share Capital	Repair Revenue
(1) 5,000	(2) 900	(8) 2,500	(5) 7,500	(1) 5,000	(3) 1,500
(5) 7,500	(8) 2,500				
(6) 500	(10) 2,000				

Accounts Receivable		Accounts Payable		Electricity Expense
(3) 1,500	(6) 500	(10) 2,000	(4) 2,000	(7) 200
			(7) 200	

Prepaid Expense		Rent Expense
(2) 900	(11) 300	(11) 300

Unused Supplies		Supplies Expense
(4) 2,000	(9) 800	(9) 800

EXERCISE 2–4

Cross Corporation
Trial Balance
At December 31, 2015

	Account Balances	
	Debits	Credits
Cash	$120,400	
Accounts Receivable	26,000	
Unused Supplies	6,000	
Land	8,000	
Building	120,000	
Accounts Payable		$30,000
Loan Payable		80,000
Share Capital		170,000
Commissions Earned		5,000
Insurance Expense	100	
Rent Expense	1,000	
Salaries Expense	3,000	
Supplies Expense	300	
Telephone Expense	200	—
Total	$285,000	$285,000

EXERCISE 2–5

General Journal				
Date	Account/Explanation	PR	Debit	Credit
	Cash		3,000	
	Share Capital			3,000
	(a) To record the issuance of share capital.			
	Equipment		2,000	
	Accounts Payable			2,000
	(b) To record the purchase of equipment on account.			
	Rent Expense		400	
	Cash			400
	(c) To record the payment of rent for the month.			
	Supplies		4,000	
	Accounts Payable			4,000
	(d) To record the purchase of supplies.			
	Accounts Receivable		2,500	
	Repair Revenue			2,500
	(e) To record repair revenue.			
	Accounts Payable		2,000	
	Cash			2,000
	(f) To record the payment on account.			
	Cash		500	
	Accounts Receivable			500
	(g) To record collection of an amount owed.			
	Cash		1,000	
	Equipment			1,000
	(h) To record the sale of equipment.			

EXERCISE 2–6

General Journal				
Date	Account/Explanation	PR	Debit	Credit
	Cash..		XX	
	Share Capital.........................			XX
	(1) To record issuance of share capital			
	Unused Supplies.........................		XX	
	Cash...............................			XX
	Accounts Payable....................			XX
	(2) To record the purchase of supplies.			
	Cash..		XX	
	Repair Revenue......................			XX
	(3) To record revenue earned.			
	Accounts receivable.....................		XX	
	Repair Revenue......................			XX
	(4) To record revenue earned.			
	Prepaid Expense.........................		XX	
	Cash...............................			XX
	(5) To record expense paid in advance.			
	Supplies Expense........................		XX	
	Accounts Payable....................			XX
	(6) To record supplies purchased and used.			
	Rent Expense............................		XX	
	Accounts Payable....................			XX
	(7) To record rent expense.			
	Cash..		XX	
	Unused Supplies....................			XX
	(8) To record the sale of supplies.			
	Electricity Expense.....................		XX	
	Prepaid Expense....................			XX
	(9) To record electricity expense for the month.			
	Accounts Payable.......................		XX	
	Cash...............................			XX
	(10) To record payment on account.			
	Cash..		XX	
	Bank Loan..........................			XX
	(11) To record the issuance of a bank loan.			

EXERCISE 2–7

a. General Ledger T-accounts with transactions:

Cash

Jan. 1	10,000	Jan. 5	200
11	1,300	4	4,000
		30	1,800
Bal.	5,300		

Accounts Receivable

Jan. 31	1,600

Unused Supplies

Jan. 9	4,000	Jan. 31	200
Bal.	3,800		

Accounts Payable

	Jan. 28	450

Share Capital

	Jan. 1	10,000

Service Revenue

	Jan. 11	1,300
	31	1,600
	Bal.	2,900

Rent Expense

Jan. 5	200

Truck Operation Expense

Jan. 28	450

Salaries Expense

Jan. 30	1,800

Supplies Expense

Jan. 31	200

b. Trial balance is as follows:

Elgert Corporation
Trial Balance
January 31, 2015

	Debit	Credit
Cash	$5,300	
Accounts receivable	1,600	
Unused supplies	3,800	
Accounts payable		$450
Share capital		10,000
Service revenue		2,900
Rent expense	200	
Truck operation expense	450	
Salaries expense	1,800	
Supplies expense	200	
Total	$13,350	$13,350

c. Income statement, statement of changes in equity, and the balance sheet are as follows:

Elgert Corporation
Income Statement
For the Month Ended January 31, 2015

Revenue		
Service revenue		$2,900
Expenses		
Rent expense	$200	
Truck operation expense	450	
Salaries expense	1,800	
Supplies expense	200	
Total expenses		2,650
Net income		$250

Elgert Corporation
Statement of Changes in Equity
For the Month Ended January 31, 2015

	Share Capital	Retained Earnings	Total Equity
Opening balance	$ 0	$ 0	$ 0
Shares issued	10,000	0	10,000
Net income	0	250	250
Ending balance	$10,000	$250	$10,250

Elgert Corporation
Balance Sheet
At January 31, 2015
Assets

Cash		$5,300
Accounts receivable		1,600
Unused supplies		3,800
Total assets		$10,700

Liabilities

Accounts payable		$450

Equity

Share capital	$10,000	
Retained earnings	250	10,250
Total liabilities and earnings		$10,700

Chapter 3 Solutions

EXERCISE 3–1

a. and **c.**

Graham Corporation
General Ledger

ASSETS	=	LIABILITIES	+	EQUITY

Interest Receivable

(a)	110	

Prepaid Insurance

	1,800		
		(b)	1,200
Bal.	600		

Interest Payable

		(c)	90

Salaries Payable

		(d)	450

Unearned Rent

			700
(e)	500		
		Bal.	200

Interest Earned

		(a)	110

Rent Earned

		(e)	500

Insurance Expense

(b)	1,200	

Interest Expense

(c)	90	

Salaries Expense

(d)	450	

b.

General Journal				
Date	Account/Explanation	PR	Debit	Credit
	Interest Receivable.....................		110	
	Interest Earned......................			110
	(a)			
	Insurance Expense.....................		1,200	
	Prepaid Insurance....................			1,200
	(b)			
	Interest Expense.......................		90	
	Interest Payable....................			90
	(c)			
	Salaries Expense.......................		450	
	Salaries Payable....................			450
	(d)			
	Unearned Rent........................		500	
	Rent Earned........................			500
	(e)			

d.

Revenues	
Interest Earned	$110
Rent Earned	500
Expenses	
Insurance Expense	$1,200
Interest Expense	90
Salaries Expense	450

EXERCISE 3–2

a. The adjustments column is as follows:

Lauer Corporation

	Trial Balance Dr.	Trial Balance Cr.	Adjustments Dr.	Adjustments Cr.	Adjusted Trial Balance Dr.	Adjusted Trial Balance Cr.
Cash	$4,000				$4,000	
Accounts Receivable	5,000				5,000	
Prepaid Insurance	3,600			(a) $300	3,300	
Prepaid Rent	1,000			(b) 500	500	
Truck	6,000				6,000	
Accumulated Depreciation – Truck				(c) 1,500		$1,500
Accounts Payable		$7,000		(d) 400		7,400
Salaries Payable				(e) 1,000		1,000
Unearned Rent		1,200	(f) $600			600
Share Capital		2,700				2,700
Revenue		25,000				25,000
Rent Earned				(f) 600		600
Advertising Expense	700				700	
Commissions Expense	2,000				2,000	
Depreciation Expense			(c) 1,500		1,500	
Insurance Expense			(a) 300		300	
Interest Expense	100		(d) 400		500	
Rent Expense	5,500		(b) 500		6,000	
Salaries Expense	8,000		(e) 1,000		9,000	
Totals	$35,900	$35,900	$4,300	$4,300	$38,800	$38,800

b. The general journal is as follows:

	General Journal			
Date	Account/Explanation	PR	Debit	Credit
	Insurance Expense		300	
	Prepaid Insurance.			300
	(a) To record expiry of prepaid insurance.			
	Rent Expense		500	
	Prepaid Rent			500
	(b) To record expiry of prepaid rent.			
	Depreciation Expense		1,500	
	Accumulated Depreciation – Truck. . . .			1,500
	(c) To record truck depreciation.			
	Interest Expense		400	
	Accounts Payable			400
	(d) To accrue interest.			
	Salaries Expense		1,000	
	Salaries Payable			1,000
	(e) To accrue unpaid salaries.			
	Unearned Rent		600	
	Rent Earned			600
	(f) To record expiry of unearned rent.			

EXERCISE 3–3

a. The general journal is as follows:

Date	General Journal Account/Explanation	PR	Debit	Credit
	Rent Expense		200	
	Prepaid Rent			200
	(a) To adjust prepaid rent account to the proper balance.			
	Office Supplies Expense		400	
	Unused Office Supplies			400
	(b) To record the ending balance of supplies on hand.			
	Income Taxes Expense		5,000	
	Income Taxes Payable			5,000
	(c) To record income taxes for the period.			
	Unearned Commissions		1,000	
	Commissions Earned			1,000
	(d) To record the proper balance in the Unearned Commissions account.			
	Salaries Expense		300	
	Salaries Payable			300
	(e) To accrue salaries for the period.			

b. Assets would be overstated by $600 [(a): 200 + (b): 400].

Liabilities would be understated by $4,300 [(c): 5,000 − (d): 1,000 + (e): 300].

Revenue would be understated by $1,000 (d).

Expenses would be understated by $5,900 [(a): 200 + (b): 400 + (c): 5,000 + (e): 300].

Equity would be overstated by $4,900 [(a):200 + (b):400 + (c):5,000 − (d):1,000 + (e):300].

EXERCISE 3–4

General Journal				
Date	Account/Explanation	PR	Debit	Credit
Dec. 31	Advertising Expense.....................		500	
	Prepaid Advertising			500
	To record the expired portion of advertising for the period.			
31	Supplies Expense		400	
	Unused Supplies....................			400
	To record the remaining amount of supplies on hand.			
31	Depreciation Expense – Equipment		250	
	Accumulated Depreciation – Equipment			250
	To record the depreciation for the period.			
31	Maintenance Expense		200	
	Telephone Expense.....................		100	
	Utilities Expense		400	
	Commissions Expense		800	
	Accounts Payable			1,500
	To record expenses incurred but not yet paid for the period.			
31	Salaries Expense		700	
	Salaries Payable			700
	To record salaries accrued for the period.			
31	Unearned Subscriptions		5,000	
	Subscription Revenue			5,000
	To record subscriptions earned for the period.			

EXERCISE 3–5

General Journal				
Date	Account/Explanation	PR	Debit	Credit
Dec. 31	Depreciation Expense – Truck		1,200	
	Accumulated Depreciation – Truck....			1,200
	To record additional truck depreciation for the year ($2,500 − 1,300) ($10,000/4 years = $2,500/year).			

EXERCISE 3–6

Interest expense for the year should be $12,000 \times 10\% = $1,200. The needed adjusting entry is:

General Journal				
Date	Account/Explanation	PR	Debit	Credit
Dec. 31	Interest Expense		100	
	Interest Payable			100
	To record interest accrued at December 31 ($1,200 − 1,100).			

EXERCISE 3–7

General Journal				
Date	Account/Explanation	PR	Debit	Credit
	Insurance Expense		600	
	Prepaid Insurance.			600
	(a) To record expiry of 6 months insurance.			
	Supplies Expense		200	
	Unused Supplies.			200
	(b) To adjust supplies on hand to physical count.			
	Telephone Expense.		50	
	Accounts Payable			50
	(c) To record account payable at year end.			

EXERCISE 3–8

Bernard Inc.
Adjusted Trial Balance
December 31, 2015

	Debits	Credits
Prepaid advertising	$1,000	
Supplies	750	
Equipment	21,750	
Accumulated depreciation – equipment		$1,500
Accounts payable		13,250
Salaries payable		700
Unearned subscriptions		10,000
Share capital		8,000
Subscription revenue		5,000
Advertising expense	500	
Commissions expense	800	
Depreciation expense – equipment	250	
Maintenance expense	200	
Salaries expense	10,200	
Supplies expense	2,500	
Telephone expense	100	
Utilities expense	400	
Totals	$38,450	$38,450

EXERCISE 3–9

General Journal				
Date	Account/Explanation	PR	Debit	Credit
Dec. 31	Commissions Earned		20,000	
	Subscriptions Revenue.		17,630	
	Income Summary			37,630
	To close revenue accounts to income summary.			
31	Income Summary		58,400	
	Depreciation Expense – Machinery . . .			900
	Depreciation Expense – Warehouse . .			1,200
	Insurance Expense			1,800
	Interest Expense			2,365
	Salaries Expense			33,475
	Supplies Expense			15,800
	Utilities Expense			2,860
	To close expense accounts to income summary.			
31	Retained Earnings		20,770	
	Income Summary			20,770
	To close net loss in income summary to retained earnings.			
31	Retained Earnings		14,000	
	Dividends			14,000
	To close dividends to retained earnings.			

Willis Inc.
Post-Closing Trial Balance
December 31, 2015

	Debits	Credits
Accounts payable		$4,400
Accounts receivable	$3,600	
Accumulated depreciation – machinery		$2,800
Accumulated depreciation – warehouse		8,000
Bank loan		47,600
Cash	12,000	
Interest payable		1,200
Land	15,000	
Machinery	20,000	
Retained earnings*		1,230
Salaries payable		1,970
Share capital		52,100
Supplies	2,500	
Unearned fees		800
Warehouse	67,000	
Totals	$120,100	$120,100

*calculated as $36,000 adjusted retained earnings balance +$37,630 total revenues closed to re-

tained earnings —$58,400 total expenses closed to retained earnings —$14,000 dividends closed to retained earnings.

Chapter 4 Solutions

EXERCISE 4–1

a. The balance sheet is as follows:

Joyes Enterprises Ltd.
Balance Sheet
At December 31, 2016

Assets

Current			
Cash		$2,000	
Accounts Receivable		8,000	
Merchandise Inventory		19,000	
Prepaid Insurance		1,000	
Total Current Assets			$30,000
Property, Plant, and Equipment			
Land		5,000	
Buildings	$25,000		
Less: Accum. Dep'n.	1,000	24,000	
Equipment	20,000		
Less: Accum. Dep'n.	4,000	16,000	
Net Property, Plant, and Equipment			45,000
Total Assets			$75,000

Liabilities

Current Liabilities		
Bank Loan	$5,000	
Accounts Payable	7,000	
Income Taxes Payable	3,000	
Total Current Liabilities		$15,000
Non-current Liabilities		
Mortgage Payable		5,000
Total Liabilities		20,000

Equity

Share Capital	48,000	
Retained Earnings	7,000	
Total Equity		55,000
Total Liabilities and Equity		$75,000

b. Current assets total $30,000. Current liabilities total $15,000. The company appears to have sufficient resources to meet its obligations in the next year.

c. Total equity is $55,000. Total liabilities equal $20,000. The ratio is $55,000/20,000 = 2.75 to 1.

EXERCISE 4–2

a. The building should likely be a non-current asset, as its useful life is generally greater than one fiscal year. Short-term investments are current assets because they are readily marketable, by definition. Unused office supplies are likely current assets, as they will usually be used in the next fiscal. The bank loan payable is due in 2022 and therefore a non-current liability, as it will not be paid within the next fiscal year. Salaries payable is likely a current liability, as it will be paid in the next fiscal year in all likelihood. The last line on the balance sheet should read "Total Liabilities and Equity". The balance sheet lists a building account but not a land account. Sometimes a company owns a building without owning land, but it is more likely that these two assets should have been separated when they were acquired. Retained earnings should be shown in the equity section. There is no accumulated depreciation recorded for the long-lived assets and there are no income taxes payable recorded. The reasons for these omissions should be investigated.

b. The balance sheet is as follows:

Abbey Limited
Balance Sheet
At November 30, 2015

Assets

Current
Cash	$1,000	
Short-term Investments	3,000	
Accounts Receivable	6,000	
Merchandise Inventory	3,000	
Unused Supplies	100	
Total Current Assets		$13,100

Property, Plant, and Equipment
Building*	12,000	
Equipment	1,500	
Truck	1,350	
Net Property, Plant, and Equipment		14,850
Total Assets		$27,950

Liabilities

Current
Accounts Payable	$5,600	
Notes Payable	2,000	
Salaries Payable	250	
Total Current Liabilities		$7,850

Non-current
Bank Loan	1,000	
Mortgage Payable	7,000	
Total Non-current Liabilities		8,000
Total Liabilities		15,850

Equity

Share Capital	11,100	
Retained Earnings	1,000	
Total Equity		12,100
Total Liabilities and Equity		$27,950

Land may need to be separated out.

c. Additional disclosure should be considered for:

- depreciation rates for plant and equipment.

- details about cost and accumulated depreciation amounts for property, plant, and equipment.

- details about debt, including interest rates, due dates, any assets securing the debt, repayment amounts and intervals, and when terms will be re-negotiated.
- details about share capital.

Chapter 5 Solutions

EXERCISE 5–1

a. The completed table is as follows:

	2014	2013	2012	2011
Sales	$10,000	$9,000	$8,000	$7,000
Cost of Goods Sold	7,500	6,840	6,160	5,460
Gross Profit	2,500	2,160	1,840	1,540
Gross Profit Percentage	25%	24%	23%	22%

b. The company's gross profit percentage has increased each year from 2011 to 2014 inclusive. This means it is earning more per sales dollar each year (from 22 cents per dollar in 2011 to 25 cents per dollar in 2014). This is a favourable trend because the company is generating more gross profit to apply against operating and other expenses which hopefully results in greater net income.

EXERCISE 5–2

General Journal					
Date	Account/Explanation	PR	Debit	Credit	
Jul. 6	Merchandise Inventory.................		600		
	Accounts Payable			600	
	To record purchase of inventory on account.				
9	Accounts Payable		200		
	Merchandise Inventory..............			200	
	To record returns made on goods purchased.				
15	Accounts Payable		400		
	Cash...............................			396	
	Merchandise Inventory..............			4	
	To record payment made within discount period.				

EXERCISE 5–3

a. The Horne Inc. general journal is as follows:

	General Journal			
Date	Account/Explanation	PR	Debit	Credit
May 5	Accounts Receivable		4,000	
	Sales			4,000
	Cost of Goods Sold		2,500	
	Merchandise Inventory			2,500
7	Sales Returns and Allowances		500	
	Accounts Receivable			500
	Merchandise Inventory		300	
	Cost of Goods Sold			300
15	Cash		3,430	
	Sales Discounts		70	
	Accounts Receivable			3,500
31	Cost of Goods Sold		100	
	Merchandise Inventory			100
	(3,000 beginning MI − 2,500 + 300 = 800 unadjusted MI balance; 800 − 700 = 100 shrinkage)			

b. The Sperling Renovations Ltd. general journal is as follows:

	General Journal			
Date	Account/Explanation	PR	Debit	Credit
May 5	Merchandise Inventory		4,000	
	Accounts Payable			4,000
7	Accounts Payable		500	
	Merchandise Inventory			500
15	Accounts Payable		3,500	
	Merchandise Inventory			70
	Cash			3,430
	The shrinkage adjustment recorded by Horne Inc. does not impact Sperling in any way therefore no adjusting entry is required in Sperling's records.			

EXERCISE 5–4

a. The income statement is as follows:

Smith Corp.
Income Statement
Year Ended June 30, 2015

Sales		$72,000
Less: Sales returns and allowances		2,000
Net sales		$70,000
Cost of goods sold		50,000
Gross profit		$20,000
Operating expenses:		
Selling expenses:		
Advertising expense	$1,500	
Commissions expense	4,000	
Delivery expense	500	
Rent expense - store	1,500	
Sales salaries expense	2,000	
Total selling expenses		$9,500
General and administrative expenses:		
Depreciation expense - equipment	500	
Insurance expense	1,000	
Office salaries expense	3,000	
Rent expense - office	1,000	
Total general and administrative expenses		5,500
Total operating expenses		15,000
Income before income tax expense		5,000
Income tax expense		1,000
Net income		$4,000

b. The gross profit percentage, rounded to two decimal places, is 28.57% calculated as $100 \times$ (20,000/70,000).

EXERCISE 5–5

a. Closing entries:

	General Journal			
Date	Account/Explanation	PR	Debit	Credit
June 30	Sales....................................		72,000	
	Income Summary....................			72,000
	(to close credit balance temporary accounts)			
30	Income Summary......................		68,000	
	Sales Returns and Allowances........			2,000
	Cost of Goods Sold...................			50,000
	Advertising Expense.................			1,500
	Commissions Expense...............			4,000
	Delivery Expense			500
	Rent Expense – Store................			1,500
	Sales Salaries Expense..............			2,000
	Depreciation Expense – Equipment...			500
	Insurance Expense..................			1,000
	Office Salaries Expense..............			3,000
	Rent Expense – Office			1,000
	Income Tax Expense.................			1,000
	(to close debit balance temporary accounts)			
30	Income Summary		4,000	
	Retained Earnings...................			4,000
	(to close balance in Income Summary to Retained Earnings)			
30	Retained Earnings.....................		2,000	
	Dividends			2,000
	(to close Dividends to Retained Earnings)			

b. The June 30, 2015 post-closing balance in Retained Earnings is $20,000 calculated as:

Retained Earnings

		18,000	Beginning Balance
Dividends	2,000	4,000	Net Income
		20,000	Ending Balance

EXERCISE 5–6

	A	B	C	D
Opening Inventory	500	184	112	750
Purchases	1,415	344	840	5,860
Transportation-In	25	6	15	10
Cost of Goods Available for Sale	1,940	534	967	6,620
Ending Inventory	340	200	135	880
Cost of Goods Sold	1,600	334	832	5,740

EXERCISE 5–7

Opening Inventory	375
Purchases	2,930
Less: Purchases Discounts	5
Less: Purchases Returns and Allowances	20
Transportation-In	105
Less: Ending Inventory	440
Cost of Goods Sold	2,945

EXERCISE 5–8

a. The completed table is as follows:

	A	B	C	D
Sales	$300	$150	$195	$90
Opening Inventory	80	40	40	12
Purchases	240	120	150	63
Cost of Goods Available for Sale	320	160	190	75
Ending Inventory	(120)	(60)	(60)	(15)
Cost of Goods Sold	200	100	130	60
Gross Profit	$100	$50	$65	$30
Gross Profit percentage	33.33%	33.33%	33.33%	33.33%

b. All four companies have the same gross profit percentage of 33.33% which means each is contributing equally to operating expenses. In terms of real dollars, Company A is doing the best because its gross profit is $100.

Chapter 6 Solutions

EXERCISE 6–1

Date		Purchased (Sold) Units		Unit Cost	COGS	Balance Units		Unit Cost		Total Cost
Jan. 1	Opening Inventory					100	×	$1	=	$100
7	Purchase #1	10	×	$2		{100 10	× ×	1 2}		120
9	Sale #1	(80)	×	1	($80)	{20 10	× ×	1 2}		40
21	Purchase #2	20	×	3		{20 10 20	× × ×	1 2 3}		100
24	Sale #2	{(20) (10) (10)	× × ×	1 2 3}	(70)	10	×	3	=	30
	Total COGS				$150					

EXERCISE 6–2

Date		Purchased (Sold) Units		Unit Cost	COGS	Balance Units		Unit Cost		Total Cost
Jan. 1	Opening Inventory					100	×	$1	=	$100
7	Purchase #1	10	×	$2		{100 10	× ×	1 2}		120
9	Sale #1	(72) (8)	× ×	1 2	($72) ($16)	{28 2	× ×	1 2}		32
21	Purchase #2	20	×	3		{28 2 20	× × ×	1 2 3}		92
24	Sale #2	{(23) (17)	× ×	1 3}	(74)	{5 2 3	× × ×	1 2 3}	=	18
	Total COGS				$162					

EXERCISE 6–3

Weighted Average (per unit costs must be rounded to two decimal places)

Date		Units	Unit Cost	COGS	Units	Unit Cost	Total Cost
			Purchased (Sold)			**Balance**	
Jan. 1	Opening Inventory				2,000	$0.50 =	$1,000
5	Sales #1	(1,200) ×	$0.50	($600)	800		400
6	Purchase #1	1,000 ×	2.00		1,800	1.33[1]	2,400
10	Purchase #2	500 ×	1.00		2,300	1.26[2]	2,900
16	Sale #2	(2,000) ×	1.26 =	(2,520)	300		380
21	Purchase #3	1,000 ×	2.50		1,300	2.22[3]	**$2,880**

[1][$400 + (1,000 × $2)]/(800 + 1,000) = $1.33/unit (rounded) [2][$2,400 + (500 × 1)]/(1,800 + 500) = $1.26/unit (rounded) [3][$380 + (1,000 × 2.50)]/(300 + 1,000) = $2.22/unit (rounded)

a. The entry for the January 5 sale:

	General Journal			
Date	Account/Explanation	PR	Debit	Credit
Jan. 5	Accounts Receivable		6,000	
	Sales			6,000
	Cost of Goods Sold		600	
	Merchandise Inventory			600
	To record Jan. 5 sales: 1,200 units × $5.00/unit selling price = $6,000.			

b. The entry for the January 16 sale:

	General Journal			
Date	Account/Explanation	PR	Debit	Credit
Jan. 16	Accounts Receivable		12,000	
	Sales			12,000
	Cost of Goods Sold		2,520	
	Merchandise Inventory			2,520
	To record Jan. 16 sales: 2,000 units × $6.00/unit selling price = $12,000.			

c. Per the above table, there are 1,300 units on hand @ $2.22 (rounded), for a total ending inventory cost of $2,880. Be careful to note that the total ending inventory cost of $2,880 is **NOT** calculated as 1,300 units × the average unit cost of $2.22. The $2,880 is calculated as the inventory balance of $380 on January 16 plus the January 21 purchase of $2,500.

EXERCISE 6–4

N/E = No Effect; O = Overstated; U = Understated

| | 2016 Statements | | | | 2017 Statements | | | |
Errors	Opening Invent.	Ending Invent.	2016 Total Assets	2016 Net Income	Opening Invent.	Ending Invent.	2017 Total Assets	2017 Net Income
1. Goods purchased in 2016 were included in the December 31, 2016 inventory, but the transaction was not recorded until early 2017.	N/E	U	U	U	U	N/E	N/E	O
2. Goods purchased in 2017 were included in December 31, 2016 inventory, and the transaction was recorded in 2016.	N/E	O	O	O	O	N/E	N/E	U

EXERCISE 6–5

a. i. Ending inventory for 2021 was understated by $2,000. Thus, cost of goods sold should have been $18,000 and gross profit, $12,000. Because of this mistake, the 2022 opening inventory was also understated by $2,000, causing cost of goods sold to be understated by $2,000 and gross profit overstated by $2,000; gross profit in 2022 should have been $15,000. There is no impact on 2023 as a result of the error.

ii. The 2023 ending inventory was overstated by $5,000. Thus, cost of goods sold should have been $30,000 and gross profit, $20,000. This error does not impact 2021 or 2022.

b. For 2021, the merchandise inventory on the balance sheet was understated by $2,000. Thus, the total assets were $2,000 less than they should have been. For 2022, there is no effect on the balance sheet, as the error is in opening inventory. For 2023, the ending inventory in the balance sheet is overstated by $5,000, which means that total assets were overstated by $5,000.

EXERCISE 6–6

a. LCNRV on a unit-by-unit basis: $(2 \times \$50) + (3 \times \$75) + (4 \times \$20) = \$405$

Therefore, LCNRV = $405 on a unit-by-unit basis.

b. LCNRV on a group inventory basis: Total cost of the group: $(2 \times \$50) + (3 \times \$150) + (4 \times \$25) = \$650$ Total NRV of the group: $(2 \times \$60) + (3 \times \$75) + (4 \times \$20) = \$425$

Therefore, LCNRV = $425 on a group inventory basis.

EXERCISE 6–7

a. Estimated amount of inventory lost in the fire:

Sales		$300,000	100%
Cost of Goods Sold:			
Opening Inventory	$80,000		
Purchases	150,000		
Cost of Goods Available	230,000		
Ending Inventory (estimated)	(iii)		
Cost of Goods Sold		(ii)	65%
Gross Profit		(i)	35%

(i)   Gross Profit   = 35% of Sales
$\qquad$ = 35% × $300,000
$\qquad$ = $105,000

(ii)   Cost of Goods Sold   = Sales − Gross Profit
$\qquad$ = $300,000 − 105,000
$\qquad$ = $195,000

(iii)   Estimated Ending Inventory   = Cost of Goods Available − Total Cost of Goods Sold
$\qquad$ = $230,000 − 195,000
$\qquad$ = $35,000

b. Balton lost about $35,000 of inventory in the fire and is claiming $45,000. This does not appear reasonable.

EXERCISE 6–8

a. Merchandise inventory turnover for each of the years 2022 to 2025:

	2025	2024	2023	2022	2021
Cost of Goods Sold	370,000	400,000	420,000	440,000	450,000
Merchandise Inventory	120,000	111,250	88,750	111,250	88,750
Merchandise Inventory Turnover	3.2	4	4.2	4.4	

b. The change in Able Corp.'s Merchandise Inventory Turnover ratio is unfavourable because inventory is being sold at a slower rate from 2022 to 2025, from 4.4 times per year in 2022 to 3.2 times per year in 2025.

Chapter 7 Solutions

EXERCISE 7–1

General Journal				
Date	Account/Explanation	PR	Debit	Credit
Mar. 1	Petty Cash.............................		200	
	Cash.................................			200
12	Office Supplies Expense..................		60	
	Maintenance Expense....................		35	
	Miscellaneous Selling Expense...........		25	
	Cash.................................			120
18	Petty Cash.............................		200	
	Cash.................................			200
25	Office Supplies Expense..................		75	
	Delivery Expense.......................		30	
	Cash.................................			105
28	Cash....................................		50	
	Petty Cash..........................			50

EXERCISE 7–2

Ferguson Corp.
Bank Reconciliation
At December 31, 2016

Cash per general ledger, Dec. 31	$5,005	Cash per bank statement, Dec. 31	$7,000
Add: Note collected by bank	1,300	*Add*: Error Fluet Inc. cheque	200
Interest on note	25	Outstanding deposit	700
Less: Bank service charges	(30)	*Less*: Outstanding cheques	(1,600)
Adjusted Cash balance, Dec. 31	$6,300	Adjusted Cash balance, Dec. 31	$6,300

Adjusting entries resulting from bank reconciliation:

General Journal				
Date	Account/Explanation	PR	Debit	Credit
Dec. 31	Cash....................................		1,325	
	Note Receivable.....................			1,300
	Interest Earned.....................			25
	To record the note collected by the bank.			
31	Interest and Bank Charges Expense......		30	
	Cash.................................			30
	To record service charges from the bank.			

OR

General Journal				
Date	Account/Explanation	PR	Debit	Credit
Dec. 31	Cash....................................		1,295	
	Interest and Bank Charges Expense		30	
	Note Receivable			1,300
	Interest Earned			25
	To record bank service charges and note collected by the bank.			

EXERCISE 7–3

Gladstone Ltd.

Bank Reconciliation

At March 31, 2018

Cash per general ledger, Mar. 31	$2,531	Cash per bank statement, Mar. 31	$1,500
Add: Error cheque No. 4302	27	Add: Outstanding deposit	1,000
Note receivable	250	Error re. Global	250
Interest on note	50		
Less: Service charges – March	(20)	Less: Outstanding cheques	(622)
Service charges – Note	(10)		
NSF cheque	(700)		
Adjusted Cash balance, Mar. 31	$2,128	Adjusted Cash balance, Mar. 31	$2,128

Adjusting entries:

General Journal				
Date	Account/Explanation	PR	Debit	Credit
Mar. 31	Cash....................................		27	
	Office Supplies Expense			27
	To correct ck. no. 4302			
	Cash....................................		290	
	Interest and Bank Charges Expense		10	
	Note Receivable			250
	Interest Earned			50
	To record note collected by the bank.			
	Interest and Bank Charges Expense		20	
	Cash................................			20
	To record service charges for March.			
	Accounts Receivable		700	
	Cash................................			700
	To record NSF cheque returned.			

OR

General Journal				
Date	Account/Explanation	PR	Debit	Credit
Mar. 31	Interest and Bank Charges Expense		30	
	Accounts Receivable		700	
	Office Supplies Expense			27
	Note Receivable			250
	Interest Earned			50
	Cash.............................			403
	To record adjustments resulting from March 31, 2018 bank rec.			

EXERCISE 7–4

a. i. Entry to record the estimated uncollectible accounts at December 31, 2015:

General Journal				
Date	Account/Explanation	PR	Debit	Credit
	Bad Debt Expense.....................		15,000	
	Allowance for Doubtful Accounts.....			15,000
	(2% × 750,000 = 15,000)			

ii. Allowance for Doubtful Accounts = 3,000 + 15,000 = 18,000

b. i. Entry to record the estimated uncollectible accounts at December 31, 2015:

General Journal				
Date	Account/Explanation	PR	Debit	Credit
	Bad Debt Expense.....................		11,700	
	Allowance for Doubtful Accounts.....			11,700
	[10% × 147,000] = 14,700 − 3,000 = 11,700			

ii. Allowance for Doubtful Accounts = 3,000 + 11,700 = 14,700
(or 10% × 147,000)

c. There is a difference in the estimates because different methods are used. The first method is based on a percentage of sales; the second on percentage of accounts receivable, a simplified balance sheet method.

d. The calculation made in part (a) above better matches revenues and expenses: the revenues (sales) is directly related to the amount that is written off as bad debt expense. The calculation made in part (b) above better matches accounts receivable to allowance for doubtful accounts and thus produces a better balance sheet valuation.

EXERCISE 7–5

a. Amount of bad debt expense in 2019:

Allowance for doubtful accounts, Dec. 31, 2018	$8,000
Written off in 2019	(2,400)
	5,600
Allowance for doubtful accounts, Dec. 31, 2019	(9,000)
Bad debt expense for 2019	$3,400

OR

Allowance for Doubtful Accounts

		8,000	Dec. 31/18 Adj. Bal
2019 A/R Write-Offs	2,400		
		?	Adj. Entry Dec. 31/19
		9,000	Dec. 31/19 Adj. Bal.

b. Entry recorded at December 31, 2019 to account for bad debts:

	General Journal			
Date	Account/Explanation	PR	Debit	Credit
Dec. 31	Bad Debt Expense.....................		3,400	
	Allowance for Doubtful Accounts.....			3,400

c. Amount of bad debt expense in 2020:

Allowance for doubtful accounts, Dec. 31, 2019	$ 9,000
Written off in 2020	(1,000)
Recovered in 2020	300
	8,300
Allowance for doubtful accounts, Dec. 31, 2020	(10,000)
Bad debt expense for 2020	$ 1,700

OR

Allowance for Doubtful Accounts

		9,000	Dec. 31/19 Adj. Bal.
2020 A/R Write-Offs	1,000	300	2020 Recovery
		?	Adj. Entry Dec. 31/20
		10,000	Dec. 31/20 Adj. Bal.

Recall that the ending balance in one period becomes the beginning balance in the next.

d. Entry recorded at December 31, 2020 to account for bad debts:

	General Journal			
Date	Account/Explanation	PR	Debit	Credit
Dec. 31	Bad Debt Expense.....................		1,700	
	Allowance for Doubtful Accounts.....			1,700

EXERCISE 7–6

Part a:

	General Journal			
Date	Account/Explanation	PR	Debit	Credit
Mar. 1	Notes Receivable – West Corp.		40,000.00	
	Accounts Receivable – West Corp.			40,000.00
	To record 90-day, 3% note receivable.			
31	Interest Receivable		98.63	
	Interest Revenue (or Interest Earned) .			98.63
	To record accrued interest; 40,000 × 3% × 30/365.			
May 30	Cash		40,295.89	
	Interest Receivable			98.63
	Interest Revenue (or Interest Earned) .			197.26
	Notes Receivable – West Corp.			40,000.00
	To record collection; 40,000 × 3% × 60/365 = 197.26.			
Jun. 15	Notes Receivable – Jill Monte		50,000.00	
	Accounts Receivable – Jill Monte			50,000.00
	To record 45-day, 3% note receivable.			
Jul.30*	Cash		50,184.93	
	Notes Receivable – Jill Monte			50,000.00
	Interest Revenue (or Interest Earned) .			184.93
	To record collection; 50,000 × 3% × 45/365.			

*July 30 is determined by: June 30 − June 15 = 15 days + 30 days in July = 45 days.

Part b:

	General Journal			
Date	Account/Explanation	PR	Debit	Credit
May 30	Notes Receivable – West Corp.*		40,295.89	
	Interest Receivable			98.63
	Interest Revenue (or Interest Earned) .			197.26
	Notes Receivable – West Corp.			40,000.00
	To record dishonoured note; 40,000 × 3% × 60/365 = 197.26.			

*When a note is dishonoured, a 'new' note is recorded that includes the interest and principal to be recovered.

EXERCISE 7–7

a. Acid test ratio

2017: $(30,000 + 20,000)/(12,000 + 8,000 + 9,000) = 1.72$

2018: $(42,000 + 25,000)/(14,000 + 9,000 + 11,000 + 17,000) = 1.31$

Accounts receivable turnover ratio

2017: $367,000/[(20,000 + 14,000)/2] = 21.59$

2018: $375,000/[(25,000 + 20,000)/2] = 16.67$

b. The change in both the acid-test and accounts receivable turnover ratios was unfavourable. Although Salzl Corp.'s acid-test is greater than one indicating that it has sufficient quick current assets to cover current liabilities as they come due, that amount decreased from 2017 to 2018. The decrease in the accounts receivable turnover indicates that Salzl Corp. Is collecting receivables at a much slower rate in 2018 than in 2017 which is unfavourable. Receivables should be collected as quickly as possible so the accounts receivable turnover ratio should be as high as possible.

Chapter 8 Solutions

EXERCISE 8–1

f	Battery purchased for truck.
a	Commission paid to real estate agent to purchase land.
c	Cost of equipment test runs.
b	Cost to remodel building.
b or c	Cost to replace manual elevator with automatic elevator.
a	Cost of sewage system.
c	Equipment assembly expenditure.
c	Expenditures for debugging new equipment and getting it ready for use.
e	Installcation of air-conditioner in automobile.
b	Insurance paid during construction of building.
a	Legal fees associated with purchase of land.
f	Oil change for truck.
a	Payment for landscaping.
a	Expenditures for removal of derelict structures.
f	Repair made to building after moving in.
f	Repair of collision damage to truck.
f	Repair of torn seats in automobile.
e	Replacement of engine in automobile.
c	Special floor foundations for installation of new equipment.
f	Tires purchased for truck.
c	Transportation expenditures to bring newly purchased equipment to plant.

EXERCISE 8–2

	General Journal			
Date	Account/Explanation	PR	Debit	Credit
	Land....................................		75,000	
	Building...............................		225,000	
	Cash................................			300,000
	Land = $100,000/$400,000 × $300,000			
	= $75,000.			
	Building = $300,000/$400,000 ×			
	$300,000 = $225,000.			

EXERCISE 8–3

a. Cost = $3,575 + $100 + $350 = $4,025.

b. Straight-Line Method:

Year	Straight-Line	Double-Declining Balance
1	$755*	$4,025 × 40%** = $1,610
2	$755	2,415 × 40% = 966
3	$755	1,449 × 40% = 580
4	$755	869 × 40% = 348
5	$755	521 × 40% = 208

* ($4,025 − 250)/5 years = $755

** (Rate = $2/n$ where n = useful life; 2/5yrs. = .40 or 40%)

Under the straight-line method, each period is assumed to receive equal benefits from the use of the asset. Under the double-declining balance method, each period is charged a diminishing amount. The straight-line method would be more appropriate if the economic benefits would be used about equally over the years. The double-declining balance method would be better to use if the economic benefits were used up more in the first few years. The DDB method is likely the better choice, given the probability of technological obsolescence of this type of asset.

EXERCISE 8–4

a. Straight-Line Method:

($240,000 − 40,000)/5 years = $40,000 per year

2019 depreciation	=	$40,000
2020 depreciation	=	40,000
2021 depreciation	=	40,000
2022 depreciation	=	40,000
2023 depreciation	=	40,000
Total depreciation	=	$200,000*

*Maximum allowable depreciation = Cost − Residual which is $240,000 − $40,000 = $200,000.

b. Double-Declining Balance Method:

Rate = $2/n$ = 2/5 = 0.40 or 40%

2019 depreciation = $240,000 × 40% =	$ 96,000
2020 depreciation = ($240,000 − 96,000) × 40% =	57,600
2021 depreciation = ($240,000 − 96,000 × 57,600) × 40% =	34,560
2022 depreciation =	11,840*
2023 depreciation =	0
Total depreciation =	$200,000

*Maximum allowable depreciation = $200,000 which is Cost − Residual. Therefore, although the calculation of depreciation for 2022 is:

2022 depreciation = ($240,000 − 96,000 − 57,600 − 34,560) × 40% = 20,736

taking this amount would exceed the maximum allowable total depreciation of $200,000. Therefore, only $11,840 of depreciation can be recorded in 2022. This is calculated as $200,000 maximum allowable − $96,000 depreciation in 2019 − $57,600 depreciation in 2020 − $34,560 depreciation taken in 2021 = $11,840.

EXERCISE 8–5

a. Straight-Line Method:

($110,000 − 40,000)/4 years = $17,500 per year

2019 depreciation	=	$17,500
2020 depreciation	=	17,500
2021 depreciation	=	17,500
2022 depreciation	=	17,500
Total depreciation	=	$70,000*

*Maximum allowable depreciation = Cost − Residual which is $110,000 − $40,000 = $70,000.

b. Double-Declining Balance Method:

Rate $= 2/n = 2/4 = 0.50$ or 50%

2019 depreciation $= \$110,000 \times 50\% =$	$55,000
2020 depreciation $=$	15,000*
2021 depreciation $=$	0
2022 depreciation $=$	0
Total depreciation $=$	$70,000

*Maximum allowable depreciation $= \$70,000$ which is Cost $-$ Residual. Therefore, although the calculation of depreciation for 2020 is:

2020 depreciation $= (\$110,000 - 55,000) \times 50\% = \$27,500$

taking this amount would exceed the maximum allowable total depreciation of $70,000. Therefore, only $15,000 of depreciation can be recorded in 2020. This is calculated as $70,000 maximum allowable $-$ \$55,000 depreciation in 2019 $= \$15,000$.

EXERCISE 8–6

a.   i. Straight-Line Method:

($25,000 $-$ 5,000)/5 years $= \$4,000$ per year
2019 depreciation $= \$4,000 \times 1/2 = \mathbf{\$2,000}$
2020 depreciation $= \mathbf{\$4,000}$

   ii. Units-of-Production Method:

($25,000 $-$ 5,000)/500,000 km. $= \$0.04$/km.
2019 depreciation $= 120,000$ km. $\times \$0.04 = \mathbf{\$4,800}$*
2020 depreciation $= 150,000$ km. $\times \$0.04 = \mathbf{\$6,000}$

*The 1/2 year rule does not apply under usage methods of calculating depreciation since depreciation is based on units produced and not time.

   iii. Double-Declining-Balance Method:

$2/n = 2/5 = 0.40$ or 40% per year
2019 depreciation $= \$25,000 \times 40\% = \$10,000 \times 1/2$ yr. $= \mathbf{\$5,000}$
2020 depreciation $= (\$25,000 - 5,000) \times 40\% = \mathbf{\$8,000}$

b.   i. Straight-Line Method:

($25,000 $-$ 5,000)/5 years $= \$4,000$ per year
2019 depreciation $= \$4,000 \times 10/12 = \mathbf{\$3,333}$
2020 depreciation $= \mathbf{\$4,000}$

ii. Units-of-Production Method:

($25,000 − 5,000)/500,000 km. = $0.04/km.

2019 depreciation = 120,000 km. × $0.04 = **$4,800***

2020 depreciation = 150,000 km. × $0.04 = **$6,000**

*The 1/2 year rule does not apply under usage methods of calculating depreciation since depreciation is based on units produced and not time.

iii. Double-Declining-Balance Method:

$2/n = 2/5 = 0.40$ or 40% per year

2019 depreciation = $25,000 × 40% = $10,000 × 10/12 = **$8,333**

2020 depreciation = ($25,000 − 8,333) × 40% = **$6,667**

EXERCISE 8–7

	General Journal			
Date	**Account/Explanation**	**PR**	**Debit**	**Credit**
	Depreciation Expense – Machinery		3,333	
	Accumulated Depreciation – Machinery			3,333
	To record revised depreciation at Dec. 31, 2021; (60,000 − 0)/3 years = 20,000 depreciation for each of 2019 and 2020; (60,000 − 20,000 − 20,000 − 10,000)/(5 − 2) = 3,333 revised depreciation 2021			

EXERCISE 8–8

a. General journal entry to record depreciation for the year ended December 31, 2019:

	General Journal			
Date	**Account/Explanation**	**PR**	**Debit**	**Credit**
	Depreciation Expense – Machinery		28,000	
	Accumulated Depreciation – Machinery			28,000
	To record depreciation at Dec. 31, 2019; (140,000 − 0)/5 years = 28,000 depreciation for December 31, 2019			

b. General journal entry to record revised depreciation for the year ended December 31, 2020:

General Journal				
Date	Account/Explanation	PR	Debit	Credit
	Depreciation Expense – Machinery		40,500	
	Accumulated Depreciation – Machin-ery			40,500
	To record revised depreciation at Dec. 31, 2020; Original Machinery: (140,000 – 0)/5 years = 28,000 depreciation; New Compo-nent: (50,000 – 0)/4 years = 12,500 de-preciation; 28,000 + 12,500 = 40,500 to-tal depreciation at December 31, 2020			

NOTE: Because of componentization, depreciation will likely be recorded on the machinery and the new component separately. Therefore, it is acceptable to record two journal entries instead of one.

EXERCISE 8–9

a. General journal entry to record any impairment losses at December 31, 2019:

General Journal				
Date	Account/Explanation	PR	Debit	Credit
	Impairment Loss		22,917	
	Machinery			22,917
	To record impairment at Dec. 31, 2019; ($400,000 Cost – $27,083 Accum. Dep. = $372,917 Carrying or Book Value) – $350,000 Recoverable Amount = $22,917 Impairment Loss			

The land's recoverable amount of $115,000 is greater than its carrying or book value of $100,000 therefore there is no impairment.

The building's recoverable amount of $870,000 is greater than its carrying or book value of $855,333 ($890,000 – $34,667) therefore there is no impairment.

b. General journal entry to record depreciation for the year ended December 31, 2020:

General Journal				
Date	Account/Explanation	PR	Debit	Credit
	Depreciation Expense – Building.........		32,000	
	Accumulated Depreciation – Building .			32,000
	To record depreciation at Dec. 31, 2020; calculated as ($890,000 − $250,000)/20 years = $32,000			
	Depreciation Expense – Machinery......		22,430	
	Accumulated Depreciation – Machinery......................................			22,430
	To record depreciation at Dec. 31, 2020; calculated as ($400,000 − $150,000 − $27,083 − $22,917)/(10 − 1 1/12 = 8 11/12 years) = $22,430. Note that the Accum. Dep. of $27,083 represents 1 year and 1 month of depreciation (1 month in 2018 + 12 months in 2019). Therefore, the remainder over which the machinery's cost must be depreciated is the original 10 years less the 1 year and 1 month.			

EXERCISE 8–10

a. Journal entries to record the exchange on the books of:

(a) Freeman:

General Journal				
Date	Account/Explanation	PR	Debit	Credit
	Equipment		200,000	
	Land...............................			125,000
	Gain on Disposal....................			75,000
	The equipment is valued at the fair value of the asset given up.			

(b) The developer:

General Journal				
Date	Account/Explanation	PR	Debit	Credit
	Land.....................................		240,000	
	Equipment.........................			325,000
	Accumulated Depreciation – Equipment..		80,000	
	Loss on Disposal		5,000	
	To record loss on disposal calculated as: [$325,000 Cost − $80,000 Accumulated Depreciation = $245,000 Carrying Amount] − [$240,000 Proceeds [fair value of equipment]] = $5,000.			

b. The developer may be speculating that the land will increase in value in the future beyond the current fair value of the equipment exchanged for the land.

EXERCISE 8–11

a. Equipment sold for $20,000:

	General Journal			
Date	Account/Explanation	PR	Debit	Credit
	Cash...................................		20,000	
	Accumulated Depreciation – Equipment..		40,000	
	Equipment.........................			60,000
	To record sale of equipment for $20,000.			

b. Equipment sold for $30,000:

	General Journal			
Date	Account/Explanation	PR	Debit	Credit
	Cash...................................		30,000	
	Accumulated Depreciation..............		40,000	
	Equipment.........................			60,000
	Gain on Disposal....................			10,000
	To record gain on disposal calculated as: [$60,000 Cost of Equipment — $40,000 Accumulated Depreciation = $20,000 Carrying Amount (or net book value)] — $30,000 Proceeds of Disposal = $(10,000).			

c. Equipment sold for $5,000:

	General Journal			
Date	Account/Explanation	PR	Debit	Credit
	Cash...................................		5,000	
	Accumulated Depreciation..............		40,000	
	Loss on Disposal......................		15,000	
	Equipment.........................			60,000
	To record loss on disposal calculated as: [$60,000 Cost of Equipment — $40,000 Accumulated Depreciation = $20,000 Carrying Amount (or net book value)] — $5,000 Proceeds of Disposal = $15,000.			

To record loss on disposal calculated as:

Cost of equipment	$60,000
Accumulated depreciation	(40,000)
Carrying amount (or net book value)	20,000
Proceeds of disposal	(5,000)
Loss on disposal	$15,000

EXERCISE 8–12

a. March 1, 2019 to record the purchase of the copyright:

	General Journal				
Date	Account/Explanation	PR	Debit	Credit
	Copyright		50,000	
	Cash.			50,000
	To record purchase of copyright.			

b. December 31, 2019, Willis's year-end, to record amortization of the copyright:

	General Journal				
Date	Account/Explanation	PR	Debit	Credit
	Amortization Expense		8,333	
	Accumulated Amortization – Copyright			8,333
	To record amortization; 50,000/5 = 10,000 × 10/12 = 8,333.			

c. October 1, 2021, Willis's sale of the copyright to a movie producer for $100,000:

	General Journal				
Date	Account/Explanation	PR	Debit	Credit
	Cash		100,000	
	Accumulated Amortization – Copyright . . .		25,833	
	Copyright			50,000
	Gain on Disposal			75,833
	To record sale of copyright at a gain; Accumulated amortization = 8,333 for 2019 + 10,000 for 2020 + 7,500 for 2021 = 25,833.			

Chapter 9 Solutions

EXERCISE 9–1

Ajam Inc.
Partial Balance Sheet
March 31, 2019

Current liabilities:		
Accounts payable	$58,000	
Wages payable	102,000	
Income taxes payable	92,000	
Note payable, due November 30, 2019	64,000	
Current portion of mortgage payable	80,000	
Total current liabilities		$396,000
Long-term liabilities:		
Note payable, due May 15, 2021	$108,000	
Long-term portion of mortgage payable	240,000	
Total long-term liabilities		348,000
Total liabilities		$744,000

EXERCISE 9–2

General Journal					
Date	Account/Explanation	PR	Debit	Credit
June 7	Accounts Receivable		56,000	
	PST Payable			3,500
	GST Payable			2,500
	Service Revenue			50,000
June 27*	Cash		56,000	
	Accounts Receivable			56,000

* The PST and GST collected on June 27 will be paid when due and recorded in a separate entry.

EXERCISE 9–3

a. Entry to record the issuance of the note on July 1, 2019:

General Journal				
Date	Account/Explanation	PR	Debit	Credit
July 1	Cash		300,000.00	
	Notes Payable			300,000.00
	To record 45-day, 3.5% note issued July 1.			

b. Entry to accrue interest on July 31, 2019:

General Journal				
Date	Account/Explanation	PR	Debit	Credit
July 31	Interest Expense		863.01	
	Interest Payable			863.01
	To record accrued interest; 300,000 × 3.5% × 30/365.			

c. August 15, 2019 (July 31 − July 1 = 30 days + August 15 = 45 days)

d. Entry to record the payment of the note on the due date:

General Journal				
Date	Account/Explanation	PR	Debit	Credit
Aug. 15	Notes Payable		300,000.00	
	Interest Payable.		863.01	
	Interest Expense		431.51	
	Cash.			301,294.52
	To record payment of note; 300,000 × 15/365 × 3.5% = 431.51.			

EXERCISE 9–4

a. Entry to record the estimated warranty liability for January:

General Journal				
Date	Account/Explanation	PR	Debit	Credit
Jan. 23	Warranty Expense.		1,640	
	Estimated Warranty Liability			1,640
	To record estimated warranty liability; 2% × $82,000 = $1,640.			

b. Entry to record the warranty expense incurred in January:

General Journal				
Date	Account/Explanation	PR	Debit	Credit
Jan. 29	Estimated Warranty Liability		2,000	
	Merchandise Inventory.			2,000
	To record replacement of furniture covered by warranty.			

c. $380 (calculated as: $640 + 1,640 − 2,000).

EXERCISE 9–5

   a. discount

   b. premium

   c. discount

   d. premium

   e. premium

   f. discount

EXERCISE 9–6

Cash = $100,000 \times 94\% = \$94,000$

Discount = $\$100,000 - \$94,000 = \$6,000$

General Journal					
Date	Account/Explanation	PR	Debit	Credit
Jan. 1	Cash...............................		94,000	
	Discount on Bonds.....................		6,000	
	Bonds Payable......................			100,000

EXERCISE 9–7

Cash = $200,000 \times 112\% = \$224,000$

Premium = $\$224,000 - \$200,000 = \$24,000$

General Journal					
Date	Account/Explanation	PR	Debit	Credit
Jan. 1	Cash...............................		224,000	
	Premium on Bonds..................			24,000
	Bonds Payable......................			200,000

EXERCISE 9–8

   a.   (a) Entry to record receipt of loan proceeds from the bank:

General Journal					
Date	Account/Explanation	PR	Debit	Credit
Jan. 1	Cash...............................		50,000	
	Loan Payable......................			50,000
	To record loan from Second Capital Bank.			

(b) Entry to record purchase of the equipment:

General Journal					
Date	Account/Explanation	PR	Debit	Credit
Jan 1	Equipment		48,000	
	Cash			48,000
	To record the purchase of equipment.			

b. The loan repayment schedule is as follows:

Rosedale Corp.
Loan Repayment Schedule

	A	B	C	D	E
			(D − B)		(A − C)
Year	Beginning	(A × 6%)	Reduction	Total	Ending
Ended	Loan	Interest	of Loan	Loan	Loan
Dec. 31	Balance	Expense	Payable	Payment	Balance
2014	$50,000	$3,000	$15,705	$18,705	$34,295
2015	34,295	2,058	16,647	18,705	17,648
2016	17,648	1,057*	17,648	18,705	-0-
			$50,000		

* Adjusted for rounding

c. Entry to record the first loan payment:

General Journal					
Date	Account/Explanation	PR	Debit	Credit
Dec. 31	Interest Expense		3,000	
	Loan Payable		15,705	
	Cash			18,705
	To record loan payment to Second Capital Bank.			

Chapter 10 Solutions

EXERCISE 10–1

a. The completed schedule is as follows:

	12% Bonds	Preferred Shares	Common Shares
Income before interest and income taxes	$12,000,000	$12,000,000	$12,000,000
Less: Interest expense	4,800,000[1]	-0-	-0-
Income before taxes	7,200,000	12,000,000	12,000,000
Less: Income taxes at 50%	3,600,000	6,000,000	6,000,000
Net income	3,600,000	6,000,000	6,000,000
Less: Preferred dividends	-0-	4,000,000[2]	-0-
Net income available to common shareholders (a)	$3,600,000	$2,000,000	$6,000,000
Number of common shares outstanding (b)	200,000	200,000	400,000
Earnings per common share (a/b)	$18	$10	$15

[1]$40,000,000 \times 12\% = $4,800,000

[2]400,000 \times $10 = $4,000,000

b. Issuing bonds is the financing option that is most advantageous to the common shareholders, all other factors being considered equal. It results in higher earnings per common share. A second advantage of issuing bonds is that it does not disrupt current shareholder control. The option to issue more shares would distribute control over a larger number of shareholders causing the control held by the present shareholders to be diluted. A third advantage of issuing bonds is that interest expense is deductible for tax purposes, while dividends are paid out of after-tax dollars. One disadvantage of issuing bonds, which may make one of the other options more advantageous, is that interest expense is fixed. Issuing bonds increases interest expense and the company must earn enough income to cover the interest expense in any given year.

EXERCISE 10–2

a. Entry to record the transaction:

	General Journal				
Date	Account/Explanation	PR	Debit	Credit
	Land....................................		50,000	
	Preferred Shares....................			50,000
	To record the purchase of a tract of land in exchange for preferred shares.			

b. The credit part of the transaction would be classified on the balance sheet in the equity section as part of share capital. The debit part of the transaction would be recorded as an asset in the property, plant, and equipment section.

EXERCISE 10–3

a. The average price received for each issued preferred share is $54 ($3,456/64).

b. The average price received for each issued common share is $2.10 ($1,680/800).

c. The total contributed capital is $5,136 ($3,456 + 1,680).

EXERCISE 10–4

a. Entry to record the declaration of the dividend:

General Journal					
Date	Account/Explanation	PR	Debit	Credit
May 25	Dividends Declared....................		100,000	
	Dividends Payable			100,000
	To record the declaration of the dividend.			

b. Entry to record the payment of the dividend:

General Journal					
Date	Account/Explanation	PR	Debit	Credit
June 26	Dividends Payable.....................		100,000	
	Cash.............................			100,000
	To record the payment of the dividend.			

EXERCISE 10–5

a. Since the preferred shareholders have cumulative shares, they must receive all dividends in arrears **and** the current dividend before the common shareholders receive any dividends.

Dividends received by preferred shareholders (1,000 shares × $5/share = $5,000/year dividend entitlement):

$$= \text{Dividends in arrears for one year} + \text{Dividends for current year}$$
$$= \$5,000 + 5,000 = \$10,000$$

Common shareholders receive the balance, or $4,000 ($14,000 − $10,000).

b. Preferred shareholders receive dividends before the common shareholders. Since the preferred shareholders are not cumulative shares, they receive only the current dividend or $5,000.

Common shareholders receive the balance, or $9,000 ($14,000 − $5,000).

EXERCISE 10–6

a. The $15,000 of dividends in arrears at December 31, 2019 does not appear as a liability. Although the dividends pertain to cumulative shares, no liability exists until the board of directors declares a dividend. However, disclosure of dividends in arrears would be made in a note to the financial statements.

b. The company may have sufficient retained earnings but may not have sufficient cash to pay the dividends, taking into consideration other needs of the company.

c. The amount available for dividends to the common shareholders is calculated as follows:

Amount available for all dividends (1/2 × $35,000)	$17,500
Priority given to cumulative preferred shareholders	
Arrears to December, 2019	(15,000)
Preferred dividends for 2020	(5,000)
Deficiency	$(2,500)

The $2,500 deficiency in 2020 preferred dividends has to be paid in the future before any dividends are paid to common shareholders. There will be no dividends available for common shareholders at December 31, 2020 based on the projections.

EXERCISE 10–7

	General Journal			
Date	Account/Explanation	PR	Debit	Credit
Apr. 1	Share Dividend Declared...............		15,000	
	Common Share Dividend To Be Distributed.............................			15,000
	To record the declaration of the share dividend. (10,000 shares × 10% = 1,000 shares × $15)			

OR

	General Journal			
Date	Account/Explanation	PR	Debit	Credit
	Retained Earnings.....................		15,000	
	Common Share Dividend To Be Distributed.............................			15,000
	To record the declaration of the share dividend. (10,000 shares × 10% = 1,000 shares × $15)			

General Journal				
Date	Account/Explanation	PR	Debit	Credit
Apr. 15	Common Share Dividend To Be Distributed		15,000	
	Common Shares			15,000
	To record the distribution of the dividend.			
Jun. 1	Cash Dividends Declared		22,000	
	Dividends Payable			22,000
	To record the declaration of the cash dividend. [(10,000 shares + 1,000 shares) × $2]			

OR

General Journal				
Date	Account/Explanation	PR	Debit	Credit
	Retained Earnings		22,000	
	Dividends Payable			22,000
	To record the declaration of the cash dividend. [(10,000 shares + 1,000 shares) × $2]			

General Journal				
Date	Account/Explanation	PR	Debit	Credit
Jun. 30	Dividends Payable		22,000	
	Cash			22,000
	To record payment of the cash dividend.			
Dec. 31	Retained Earnings		37,000	
	Share Dividend Declared			15,000
	Cash Dividend Declared			22,000
	To close the Dividends Declared general ledger account to the Retained Earnings account.			

OR

If Retained Earnings was debited on April 1 (instead of Share Dividends Declared) and June 1 (instead of Cash Dividends Declared), then no closing entry is required on December 31.

EXERCISE 10–8

a.   i. Book value per preferred share = ($300 + 30)/300 shares = $1.10 per share

     ii. Book value per common share = ($992 − 330)/20 shares = $33.10 per share

b. Book value per common share after split = $662/40 shares = $16.55 per share

---

Chapter 11 Solutions

EXERCISE 11–1

F	A payment of $5,000 was made on a bank loan.
O	Depreciation expense for equipment was $1,000.
F	$10,000 of share capital was issued for cash.
F	Cash dividends of $2,500 were declared and paid to shareholders.
NC	Bonds were issued in exchange for equipment costing $7,000.
I	Land was purchased for $25,000 cash.
O	$750 of accrued salaries was paid.
O	$10,000 of accounts receivable was collected.
NC & I	A building was purchased for $80,000: $30,000 was paid in cash and the rest was borrowed.
I	A long-term investment in shares of another company was sold for $50,000 cash.
O & I	Equipment was sold for $6,000. The related accumulation depreciation was $3,000 with an original cost of $10,000.
O	$1,200 was paid for a 12-month insurance policy in effect next year.
O	A patent was amortized for $500.
F	Bonds were issued for $50,000 cash.

EXERCISE 11–2

a. The reconstructed entry to record the sale of the machinery:

General Journal					
Date	Account/Explanation	PR	Debit	Credit
	Accumulated Depreciation		?	
	Cash		?	
	Loss on Sale of Machinery (given)		3	
	Machinery (given)			20

Accumulated Depreciation

		42	Dec. 31, Year 4 bal.
Debit regarding sale	? = 12	25	Dep. Expense, Year 5
		55	Dec. 31, Year 5 bal.

Therefore, the debit to cash in the journal entry must be 5 (20-12-3).

b. The reconstructed entry to record the purchase of machinery:

General Journal				
Date	Account/Explanation	PR	Debit	Credit
	Machinery		?	
	Cash..............................			?

Machinery

Dec. 31, Year 4 bal.	138			
Debit regarding purch.	? = 7	20	Credit regarding sale	
Dec. 31, Year 5 bal.	125			

Therefore, the debit to Machinery and credit to Cash in the entry must be 7 (138-20-125).

c. The reconstructed entry to record the declaration of dividends:

General Journal				
Date	Account/Explanation	PR	Debit	Credit
	Dividends or Retained Earnings..........		?	
	Dividends Payable			?

Retained Earnings

		81	Dec. 31, Year 4 bal.
Year 5 Net loss	2		
Year 5 Div. Declared	? = 35		
		44	Dec. 31, Year 5 bal.

Therefore, the debit to Dividends or Retained Earnings is 35 and credit to Dividends Payable 35 (81-2-44).

d. The reconstructed entry to record the payment of dividends:

General Journal				
Date	Account/Explanation	PR	Debit	Credit
	Dividends Payable.....................		?	
	Cash..............................			?

Dividends Payable

		5	Dec. 31, Year 4 bal.
Div. Paid Year 5	? = 39	35	Div. Declared Year 5
		1	Dec. 31, Year 5 bal.

Therefore, the debit to Dividends Payable is 39 and the credit to Cash 39 (5+35-1).

Calculations:

	Balance ($000s)		Change		Explanation of Change
	Year 5	Year 4			
Account	Dr. (Cr.)	Dr. (Cr.)	Dr.	Cr.	
Cash	40	22	18		
Accounts receivable	34	39		5	Decrease in accounts receivable
Merchandise inventory	150	146	4		Increase in merchandise inventory
Prepaid expenses	3	2	1		Increase in prepaids
Machinery	125	138	7	20	Purchase in machinery for cash of 7; Sold machinery for cash of 5; Loss on sale 3
Accumulated dep.	-55	-42	12	25	Depreciation expense 25
Accounts payable	-29	-31	2		Decrease in accounts payable
Dividends payable	-1	-5	39	35	Paid dividends of 39
Bonds payable	-15	-38	23		Paid bonds 23
Common shares	-208	-150		58	Issued common shares 58
			{ 2		Net loss 2
Retained earnings	-44	-81	{ 35		
Total			125	143	
Change in cash			18		Net increase in cash of 18

e. The statement of cash flows is as follows:

Larriet Inc.

Statement of Cash Flows

Year Ended December 31, Year 5

Cash flows from operating activities:		
Net loss		$(2)
Adjustments to reconcile net loss		
to cash provided by operating activities:		
Decrease in accounts receivable	5	
Increase in merchandise inventory	(4)	
Increase in prepaids	(1)	
Decrease in accounts payable	(2)	
Depreciation expense	25	
Loss on sale of machinery	3	
Net cash inflow from operating activities		$24
Cash flows from investing activities:		
Purchase of machinery	$(7)	
Sale of machinery	5	
Net cash outflow from investing activities		(2)
Cash flows from financing activities:		
Issued common shares	$58	
Paid bonds	(23)	
Paid dividends	(39)	
Net cash outflow from financing activities		(4)
Net increase in cash		$18
Cash at beginning of year		22
Cash at end of year		$40

Chapter 12 Solutions

EXERCISE 12–1

The calculation of ratios as shown by the financial statements of Stockwell Inc. for each of the three years is as follows:

a. Liquidity ratios

		2015	2014	2013
Current ratio		1.2:1	1.0:1	1.4:1
Acid-test ratio		0.59:1	0.48:1	0.74:1
Sales		210 (a)	120	100
Accounts receivable	–opening	30	20	20
	–closing	38	30	20
	–average	34 (b)	25	20
Accounts receivable Collection period (b/a × 365)		59 days	76 days	73 days
Cost of goods sold		158 (c)	80	55
Merchandise inventory	–opening	40	30	20
	–closing	60	40	30
	–average	50 (d)	35	25
Number of days of sales in inventory (d/c × 365)		116 days	160 days	166 days
Revenue operating cycle		175 days	236 days	239 days

- The company's working capital position does not appear to be satisfactory, since the liquid assets appear to be insufficient to meet current obligations. The acid-test ratio is quite low, well below 1:1. The company could obtain additional cash by issuing shares or acquiring long-term debt. Alternately, it may need to seek short-term financing like an operating loan from a bank to provide cash to pay liabilities as they become due.

- Control over accounts receivable and inventories has improved. Even though the dollar value of both of these items has increased, average sales and collection periods have declined in 2015. The liquidity ratios for 2014 as compared with 2015 and 2013 suggest that not enough attention was given during that year to investments in inventories and to the collection of accounts receivable. However, the improvements shown in 2015 indicate that better control is now being exercised over these current assets.

b. i. Financial structure

	2015	2014	2013
Debt to equity ratio	$150/230	$130/100	$50/96
	= 0.65:1	= 1.30:1	= 0.52:1

The appropriate financial structure for Stockwell Inc. cannot be adequately determined without knowledge of its industry, for instance. With the exception of 2014, Stockwell Inc.'s debt to equity ratio indicates a reliance on equity rather than debt financing due to the 2015 share issue. In 2014, however, a bond issue temporarily changed the financial structure. Market rates of interest for debt would need to be evaluated to see if there is potential for leverage (that is, if interest rates are lower than current return on total assets). If not, it is less likely that any potential for positive leverage exists. In this circumstance a weighting toward equity is reasonable.

ii. The proportion of assets provided by creditors is as follows: 2013 – 34.3% (50/146); 2014 – 56.5% (130/230), and 2015 – 39.5% (150/380).

iii. A disproportionately high percentage of debt, over 60% in both 2014 and 2015, is in current liabilities.

c. Other observations:

- The gross profit ratio has declined over the past year, even though sales have more than doubled (2015: $52/210 = 25%; 2014: $40/120 = 33%). The decrease in this ratio suggests either that selling prices were reduced in order to dispose of the increased production or that the expansion in production facilities resulted in a higher unit cost; possibly there was a combination of both.

- All funds derived from earnings during the last two years have been retained within the business, since no dividends have been paid. However, the investment in property, plant and equipment assets of $190 ($260 − 70) exceeds the $170 received on the issue of bonds and shares [$50 + (200 − 80)]. It appears that a substantial part of the funds derived from earnings have been used to finance additions to property, plant and equipment assets rather than to provide working capital. This has weakened the liquidity ratios.

(Other relevant observations are acceptable.)

EXERCISE 12–2

$$\text{Price-earnings ratio} \quad = \quad \frac{\text{Market price per share}}{\text{Earnings per share}}$$

This ratio indicates the stock market's expectations of profitability for the company. A higher P/E ratio indicates that the market expects the company to be profitable despite relatively lower net income at present. On this basis, company C is preferred.

A: $35/11 = 3.2

B: $40/5 = 8

C: $90/10 = 9

$$\text{Dividend yield} \quad = \quad \frac{\text{Dividends per share}}{\text{Market price per share}}$$

This ratio indicates what short-term cash return shareholders might expect on their investment in common shares of the company.

A: 0

B: $4/40 = 0.1$ or 10%

C: $6/90 = 0.067$ or 6.7%

The stock market indicates that company C is expected to be relatively more profitable than A or B in the future. However, if dividend yield is important to the shareholder, then company B should be chosen. On either basis, company A does not appear to be a good investment.

EXERCISE 12–3

a. Current ratio

$$= \frac{\text{Current assets}}{\text{Current liabilities}}$$

$$= \frac{\text{Cash} + \text{accounts receivable} + \text{inventory} + \text{prepaid expenses}}{\text{Current liabilities}}$$

$$= \$300/60$$

$$= 5{:}1$$

b. Return on total assets

$$= \frac{\text{Income from operations}}{\text{Average total assets}}$$

$$= \$46/620$$

$$= 7.4\%$$

c. Sales to total assets ratio

$$= \frac{\text{Net sales}}{\text{Average total assets}}$$

$$= \$240/620$$

$$= 38/7\%$$

d. Acid-test ratio

$$= \frac{\text{Quick assets}}{\text{Current liabilities}}$$

$$= \frac{\text{Cash} + \text{accounts receivable}}{\text{Current liabilities}}$$

$$= (\$72 + 88)/60$$

$$= 2.7{:}1$$

e. Times interest earned ratio

$= \dfrac{\text{Income from operations}}{\text{Interest expense}}$

$= \$46/8$

$= 5.75{:}1$

f. Earnings per common share

$= \dfrac{\text{Net income} - \text{preferred share dividends}}{\text{Number of common shares outstanding}}$

$= [\$20 - (\$60 \times 10\%)]/10 \text{ shares}$

$= \$1.40 \text{ per share}$

g. Accounts receivable collection period

$= \dfrac{\text{Average accounts receivable}}{\text{Net credit sales}} \times 365 \text{ days}$

$= \$88/(80\% \times \$240) \times 365 \text{ days}$

$= 167 \text{ days}$

h. Return on equity

$= \dfrac{\text{Net income}}{\text{Equity}}$

$= \dfrac{\text{Net income}}{\text{Preferred shares} + \text{Common shares} + \text{Retained earnings}}$

$= \$20/(60 + 250 + 100)$

$= 4.9\%$

EXERCISE 12–4

a. Horizontal analysis:

	2012 (a)	2011 (b)	Change Amount (a − b)	Change Percentage (a − b)/b
Sales	$2,520	$1,440	$+1,080	+75%
Cost of Goods Sold	1,890	960	+930	+96.9%
Gross Profit	630	480	+150	+31.3%
Other Expenses	510	430	+80	+18.6%
Net Income	$120	$50	+70	+140%

b. Although sales have increased, cost of goods sold has increased at a faster pace. However, operating expenses have increased at a slower pace, resulting in a substantially higher net income.

EXERCISE 12–5

a. Vertical analysis:

Escalade Corporation
Vertical Analysis of the Income Statements
For the Years Ending December 31, 2010–2012

	Common–Size Percentages		
	2012	*2011*	*2010*
Sales	100.0	100.0	100.0
Cost of Goods Sold	76.0	66.7	50.0
Gross Profit	24.0	33.3	50.0
Other Expenses	14.0	22.7	29.2
Net Income	10.0	10.6	20.8

b. Escalade's gross profit ratio has significantly declined over the past three years. This could be owing to the initial inefficiency of a larger plant or because of selling an increased number of units at a greatly reduced price to obtain a larger share of the market. At any rate, the reasons for this decline should be investigated further. Since other expenses have not increased proportionately, perhaps more money could be put into sales promotion to increase the number of units sold.

Chapter 13 Solutions

EXERCISE 13–1

a. The income statement is as follows:

B. White and C. Green Partnership
Income Statement
For the Year Ended December 31, 2015

Sales		$322,000
Cost of Goods Sold		160,500
Gross Profit		161,500
Operating Expenses		
Rent	36,000	
Advertising	27,200	
Delivery	9,600	
Office	12,800	
Utilities	23,300	108,900
Net Income		$ 52,600

b. The statement of changes in equity is as follows:

B. White and C. Green Partnership
Statement of Changes in Equity
For the Year Ended December 31, 2015

	White	*Green*	*Total*
Opening Balance	$20,000	$10,000	$30,000
Investments	10,000	10,000	20,000
Net Income	26,300	26,300	52,600
	56,300	46,300	102,600
Less: Withdrawals	7,000	5,000	12,000
Ending Balance	$49,300	$41,300	$90,600

c. The balance sheet is as follows:

B. White and C. Green Partnership
Balance Sheet
At December 31, 2015

Assets

Current
    Cash $41,000
      Accounts Receivable   68,400
      Inventory   27,000
    Total Assets $136,400

Liabilities

Current
    Accounts Payable $45,800

Equity

B. White, Capital $49,300
C. Green, Capital   41,300   90,600
    Total Liabilities and Equity $136,400

d. The closing entries for the year are as follows:

Date	Account/Explanation	PR	Debit	Credit
	General Journal			
	Sales.....................................		322,000	
	Income Summary...................			322,000
	Income Summary......................		269,400	
	Cost of Goods Sold..................			160,500
	Rent.................................			36,000
	Advertising.........................			27,200
	Delivery.............................			9,600
	Office...............................			12,800
	Utilities.............................			23,300
	Income Summary......................		52,600	
	B. White, Capital....................			26,300
	C. Green, Capital....................			26,300
	B. White, Capital......................		7,000	
	B. White, Withdrawals			7,000
	C. Green, Capital......................		5,000	
	C. Green, Withdrawals			5,000

EXERCISE 13–2

a. The statement of changes in equity for White's is as follows:

White's
Statement of Changes in Equity
For the Year Ended December 31, 2015

Opening Balance	$ 30,000
Investments	20,000
Net Income	52,600
	102,600
Less: Withdrawals	12,000
Ending Balance	$ 90,600

b. The statement in changes in equity for BW and CG Ltd. is as follows:

BW and CG Ltd.
Statement of Changes in Equity
For the Year Ended December 31, 2015

	Share Capital	Retained Earnings	Total
Opening Balance	$200	$29,800	$30,000
Common Shares Issued	20,000		20,000
Net Income		52,600	52,600
Dividends Declared		(12,000)	(12,000)
Ending Balance	$20,200	$70,400	$ 90,600

EXERCISE 13–3

a. The journal entry is as follows:

General Journal				
Date	Account/Explanation	PR	Debit	Credit
	Income Summary		52,600	
	B. White, Capital			32,875
	C. Green, Capital			19,725
	To allocate net income as follows: White ($52,600 × 5/8) + Green ($52,600 × 3/8) = $32,875 + 19,725 = $52,600			

b. The journal entry is as follows:

General Journal				
Date	Account/Explanation	PR	Debit	Credit
	Income Summary		52,600	
	B. White, Capital			37,760
	C. Green, Capital			14,840

To allocate net income as follows:

	White	Green	Total
Profit to be allocated			$52,600
Interest allocation:			
White: $20,000 × 10%	$ 2,000		
Green: $10,000 × 10%		$1,000	(3,000)
Balance			49,600
Salary allocation:	30,000	10,000	(40,000)
Balance			9,600
Balance allocated in profit and loss sharing ratio:			
White: $9,600 × 3/5	5,760		
Green: $9,600 × 2/5		3,840	(9,600)
Balance			$ -0-
Total allocated to partners	$37,760	$14,840	

EXERCISE 13–4

a. The journal entry is as follows:

	General Journal				
Date	Account/Explanation	PR	Debit	Credit
	Income Summary		210,000	
	Walsh, Capital			85,250
	Abraham, Capital			124,750

Calculations to allocate net income:

	Walsh	Abraham	Total
Net income to be allocated			$210,000
Interest allocation:			
Walsh: $320,000 × 10%	$32,000		
Abraham: $400,000 × 10%		$40,000	(72,000)
Balance			138,000
Salary allocation:	75,000	150,000	(225,000)
Balance			(87,000)
Balance allocated in profit and loss sharing ratio:			
Walsh: ($87,000) × 1/4	(21,750)		
Abraham: ($87,000) × 3/4		(65,250)	87,000
Balance			$ -0-
Total allocated to partners	$85,250 +	$124,750 =	$210,000

The total actually allocated of $210,000 must equal the net income initially required to be allocated of $210,000.

b. The journal entry is as follows:

	General Journal			
Date	Account/Explanation	PR	Debit	Credit
	C. Abraham, Capital		104,000	
	B. Walsh, Capital			9,000
	Income Summary			95,000

Calculations to allocate net loss:

	Walsh	Abraham	Total
Net income to be allocated			$(95,000)
Interest allocation:			
Walsh: $320,000 × 10%	$32,000		
Abraham: $400,000 × 10%		$40,000	(72,000)
Balance			(167,000)
Salary allocation:	75,000	150,000	(225,000)
Balance			(392,000)
Balance allocated in profit and loss sharing ratio:			
Walsh: ($392,000) × 1/4	(98,000)		
Abraham: ($392,000) × 3/4		(294,000)	392,000
Balance			$ -0-
Total allocated to partners	$9,000 +	$(104,000) =	$(95,000)

The total actually allocated of $210,000 must equal the net income initially required to be allocated of $210,000.

Chapter 1 Solutions

PROBLEM 1–1

Dumont Inc.
Income Statement
For the Month Ended January 31, 2015

Revenue		
Service revenue		$7,500
Expenses		
Advertising expense	$500	
Commissions expense	720	
Insurance expense	50	
Interest expense	80	
Rent expense	400	
Supplies expense	100	
Telephone expense	150	
Wages expense	2,500	
Total expenses		4,500
Net income		$3,000

Dumont Inc.
Balance Sheet
At January 31, 2015

Assets		
Cash	$1,300	
Accounts receivable	2,400	
Prepaid expenses	550	
Unused supplies	750	
Truck	9,000	
Total assets		$14,000
Liabilities		
Bank loan	$8,000	
Accounts payable	1,000	
Total liabilities		9,000
Equity		
Share capital	$2,000	
Retained earnings	3,000	
Total equity		5,000
Total liabilities and equity		$14,000

Dumont Inc.
Statement of Changes in Equity
For the Month Ended January 31, 2015

	Share Capital	Retained Earnings	Total Equity
Opening balance	$ -0-	$ -0-	$ -0-
Shares issued	2,000	-0-	2,000
Net income	-0-	3,000	3,000
Ending balance	$2,000	$3,000	$5,000

107

PROBLEM 1–2

1. The income statement and statement of changes in equity are as follows:

Laberge Sheathing Inc.
Income Statement
For the Month Ended August 31, 2015

Revenue		
Service revenue		$2,000
Expenses		
Advertising expense	$300	
Interest expense	500	
Maintenance expense	475	
Supplies expense	125	
Wages expense	2,600	
Total expenses		4,000
Net loss		$2,000

Laberge Sheathing Inc.
Balance Sheet
August 31, 2015

Assets

Cash	$400	
Accounts receivable	3,800	
Unused supplies	100	
Equipment	8,700	
Total assets		$13,000

Liabilities

Accounts payable		$7,800

Equity

Share capital	3,200	
Retained earnings	2,000	5,200
Total liabilities and equity		$13,000

Laberge Sheathing Inc.
Statement of Changes in Equity
Month Ended August 31, 2015

	Share Capital	Retained Earnings	Total Equity
Opening balance	$3,200	$4,000	$7,200
Net loss	-0-	(2,000)	(2,000)
Ending balance	$3,200	$2,000	$5,200

2. The percentage of assets financed by equity is 40% calculated as (5,200/13,000) × 100. Although part 2 of this question did not require that the percentage of assets financed by debt be calculated, it is 60% calculated as 100% − 40%.

PROBLEM 1–3

Larson Services Inc.
Transactions Worksheet
At August 31, 2015

			ASSETS			=		LIABILITIES		+		EQUITY	
	Cash	Acct. Rec.	Ppd. Exp.	Unused Supplies	Truck	=	Bank Loan	Acct. Pay	Unearned Revenue	+	Share Capital	Retained Earnings	
Aug. 1	+3,000										+3,000		
1	+10,000						+10,000						
1	-8,000				+8,000								
3	No effect												
4	-600		+600										
5	+2,000								+2,000				
7		+5,000										+5,000	Fees earned
9	-250											-250	Supplies expense
12				+500				+500					
15	+1,000	-1,000											
16	-200											-200	Advertising
20	-250							-250					
25	-2,800											-350	Rent expense
												-2,150	Salaries
												-50	Telephone
												-250	Truck operation
28	No Effect												
29		+6,000										+6,000	Fees earned
31									-500			+500	Fees earned
	$3,900	+ $10,000	+ $600	+ $500	+ $8,000	=	$10,000	+ $250	+ $1,500	+	$3,000	+ $8,250	

Assets = $23,000

Liabilities + Equity = $23,000

PROBLEM 1–4

Larson Services Inc.
Income Statement
For the Month Ended August 31, 2015

Revenues		
Fees earned		$11,500
Expenses		
Advertising expense	$200	
Rent expense	350	
Salaries expense	2,150	
Supplies expense	250	
Telephone expense	50	
Truck operation expense	250	
Total expenses		3,250
Net income		$8,250

Larson Services Inc.
Balance Sheet
At August 31, 2015

Assets

Cash	$3,900	
Accounts receivable	10,000	
Prepaid expenses	600	
Unused supplies	500	
Truck	8,000	
Total assets		$23,000

Liabilities

Bank loan	$10,000	
Accounts payable	250	
Unearned revenue	1,500	
Total liabilities		11,750

Equity

Share capital	3,000	
Retained earnings	8,250	
Total equity		11,250
Total liabilities and equity		$23,000

Larson Services Inc.
Statement of Changes in Equity
For the Month Ended August 31, 2015

	Share Capital	Retained Earnings	Total Equity
Opening balance	$ -0-	$ -0-	$ -0-
Shares issued	3,000	-0-	3,000
Net income	-0-	8,250	8,250
Ending balance	$3,000	$8,250	$11,250

Chapter 2 Solutions

PROBLEM 2–1

1. The trial balance is as follows:

Fox Creek Service Limited
Trial Balance
At October 31, 2015

	Account Balances	
	Debit	Credit
Cash	$1,000	
Accounts Receivable	6,000	
Equipment	7,000	
Truck	9,000	
Bank Loan		$5,000
Accounts Payable		9,000
Wages Payable		1,500
Share Capital		2,000
Repair Revenue		19,000
Advertising Expense	2,200	
Commissions Expense	4,500	
Insurance Expense	500	
Supplies Expense	800	
Telephone Expense	250	
Truck Operation Expense	1,250	
Wages Expense	4,000	
	$36,500	$36,500

2. The income statement and statement of changes in equity are as follows:

Fox Creek Service Limited
Income Statement
For the Year Ended October 31, 2015

Revenue		
Repair revenue		$19,000
Expenses		
Advertising expense	$2,200	
Commissions expense	4,500	
Insurance expense	500	
Supplies expens	800	
Telephone expense	250	
Truck operation expense	1,250	
Wages expense	4,000	
Total expenses		13,500
Net income		$ 5,500

Fox Creek Service Limited
Statement of Changes in Equity
For the Year Ended October 31, 2015

	Share Capital	Retained Earnings	Total Equity
Opening Balance	$ -0-	$ -0-	$ -0-
Shares Issued	2,000	-0-	2,000
Net Income	-0-	5,500	5,500
Ending Balance	$2,000	$5,500	$7,500

3. The balance sheet is as follows:

Fox Creek Service Limited
Balance Sheet
At October 31, 2015

Assets

Cash	$ 1,000
Accounts receivable	6,000
Equipment	7,000
Truck	9,000
Total assets	$23,000

Liabilities

Bank loan	$5,000	
Accounts payable	9,000	
Wages payable	1,500	15,500

Equity

Share capital	2,000	
Retained earnings	5,500	7,500
Total liabilities and equity		$23,000

PROBLEM 2–2

1. The general journal is as follows:

General Journal				
Date	Account/Explanation	PR	Debit	Credit
May 1	Cash....................................		5,000	
	Share Capital.......................			5,000
	To record issuance of share capital.			
5	Accounts Receivable...................		3,000	
	Service Revenue....................			3,000
	To record billings to customers.			
6	Cash....................................		2,000	
	Service Revenue....................			2,000
	To record cash payment by customers for work completed.			
10	Cash....................................		1,500	
	Accounts Receivable...............			1,500
	To record collections on account.			
11	Equipment.............................		2,000	
	Cash...............................			1,000
	Accounts Payable...................			1,000
	To record purchase of equipment partially paid by cash, remainder on account.			
15	Cash....................................		1,200	
	Accounts Receivable...............			1,200
	To record payment received on account.			
16	Prepaid Advertising....................		500	
	Cash...............................			500
	To record payment of advertising in advance.			
18	Accounts Receivable...................		2,500	
	Service Revenue....................			2,500
	To record billings to customers.			
20	Unused Supplies.......................		300	
	Cash...............................			300
	To record purchase of supplies for inventory.			
21	Cash....................................		800	
	Equipment.........................			800
	To record sale of equipment at cost.			
22	Accounts Payable......................		600	
	Cash...............................			600
	To record payment of amounts owing.			
23	Telephone Expense.....................		150	
	Accounts Payable...................			150
	To record receipt of telephone bill.			
24	Commissions Expense..................		1,100	
	Accounts Payable...................			1,100
	To record receipt of commissions bill.			
28	Rent Expense..........................		400	
	Cash...............................			400
	To record payment of rent for May.			
29	Salaries Expense.......................		3,500	
	Cash...............................			3,500
	To record payment of wages incurred.			
30	Supplies Expense......................		100	
	Unused Supplies...................			100
	To record supplies used during the month.			
31	Advertising Expense...................		250	
	Prepaid Advertising................			250
	To record expiry of prepaid advertising.			

2. The Trial Balance is as follows:

Davidson Tools Rentals Corporation
Trial Balance
May 31, 2015

	Account Balances	
	Debit	*Credit*
Cash	$4,200	
Accounts Receivable	2,800	
Prepaid Advertising	250	
Unused Supplies	200	
Equipment	1,200	
Accounts Payable		$1,650
Share Capital		5,000
Service Revenue		7,500
Advertising Expense	250	
Commissions Expense	1,100	
Rent Expense	400	
Supplies Expense	100	
Salaries Expense	3,500	
Telephone Expense	150	–
	$14,150	$14,150

Cash 101

5,000	1,000
2,000	500
1,500	300
1,200	600
800	400
—	3,500
Bal. 4,200	

Accounts Receivable 110

3,000	1,500
2,500	1,200
Bal. 2,800	

Prepaid Advertising 160

500	250
Bal. 250	

Unused Supplies 173

300	100
200	
Bal. 200	

Equipment 183

2,000	800
Bal. 1,200	

Accounts Payable 210

600	1,000
	150
	1,100
	Bal. 1,650

Share Capital 320

	5,000

Service Revenue 460

	3,000
	2,000
	2,500
	Bal. 7,500

Advertising Expense 610

250	

Commissions Expense 615

1,100	

Rent Expense 654

400	

Salaries Expense 656

3,500	

Supplies Expense 668

100	

Telephone Expense 669

150	

PROBLEM 2–3

General Journal				
Date	Account/Explanation	PR	Debit	Credit
Apr. 2015	Cash		2,000	
	Accounts receivable			2,000
	(a) To record a collection on account.			
	Accounts Receivable		3,000	
	Service Revenue			3,000
	(b) To record billings to customers.			
	Advertising Expense		300	
	Salaries Expense		2,000	
	Telephone Expense		100	
	Cash			2,400
	(c) To record payment of expenses incurred.			
	Accounts payable		1,000	
	Cash			1,000
	(d) To record payment made on account.			
	Truck Operation Expense		500	
	Accounts Payable			500
	(e) To record bill received for truck repair expense.			
	Cash		2,500	
	Accounts Receivable			2,500
	(f) To record payment received on account.			
	Accounts Receivable		1,500	
	Service revenue			1,500
	(g) To record billings to customers.			
	Rent Expense		500	
	Prepaid Rent			500
	(h) To record expiry of a portion of prepaid rent.			
	Supplies Expense		150	
	Unused Supplies			150
	(i) To record supplies used, based on count of unused supplies at end of month.			

PROBLEM 2–4

General Journal				
Date	Account/Explanation	PR	Debit	Credit
Aug. 1	Cash		3,000	
	Share Capital			3,000
	To record issuance of share capital.			
1	Cash		10,000	
	Bank Loan			10,000
	To record amount borrowed from bank.			
1	Truck		8,000	
	Cash			8,000
	To record purchase of a used truck.			
4	Prepaid Insurance		600	
	Cash			600
	To record payment of a one-year insurance policy.			
5	Cash		2,000	
	Fees Earned			2,000
	To record collection of cash fees from a customer.			
7	Accounts Receivable		5,000	
	Fees Earned			5,000
	To record billings to customers.			
9	Supplies Expense		250	
	Cash			250
	To record payment of supplies used.			
12	Unused Supplies		500	
	Accounts Payable			500
	To record purchase of supplies on account.			
15	Cash		1,000	
	Accounts Receivable			1,000
	To record collection of customer accounts.			
16	Advertising Expense		200	
	Cash			200
	To record payment of advertising expense.			
20	Accounts Payable		250	
	Cash			250
	To record payment made on account.			
25	Rent Expense		350	
	Salaries Expense		2,150	
	Telephone Expense		50	
	Truck Operation Expense		250	
	Cash			2,800
	To record cash payment of expenses.			
29	Accounts Receivable		6,000	
	Fees Earned			6,000
	To record billings to customers.			
31	Insurance Expense		50	
	Prepaid Insurance			50
	To record insurance expired for August ($600/12 months).			
31	Supplies Expense		400	
	Unused Supplies			400
	To record supplies used; $500 purchased on Aug. 12 less $100 still on hand.			

NOTE: *No entry is recorded for August 28 because a transaction did not occur.*

Chapter 3 Solutions

PROBLEM 3–1

General Journal				
Date	Account/Explanation	PR	Debit	Credit
	Rent Expense		300	
	Prepaid Rent			300
	(a) To record rent expense at year end.			
	Wages Expense		200	
	Wages Payable			200
	(b) To record accrued wages at year-end.			
	Income Taxes Expense		1,000	
	Income Taxes Payable			1,000
	(c) To record income taxes.			
	Unearned Commissions Revenue		1,000	
	Commissions Earned			1,000
	(d) To record commissions earned at year-end.			
	Other Unearned Revenue		5,000	
	Revenue			5,000
	(e) To adjust unearned revenue to actual at year end.			
	Prepaid Advertising		1,500	
	Advertising Expense			1,500
	(f) To correct advertising expense and record prepaid advertising at year-end.			
	Depreciation Expense – Equipment		500	
	Accumulated Depreciation – Equipment			500
	(g) To record depreciation expense.			
	Unused Supplies		225	
	Supplies Expense			225
	(h) To correct supplies expense and adjust for unused supplies.			
	Truck Expense		500	
	Accounts Payable			500
	(i) To record accounts payable at year-end.			

PROBLEM 3–2

	General Journal			
Date	Account/Explanation	PR	Debit	Credit
	Unused Supplies		100	
	Supplies Expense			100
	(a)			
	Telephone Expense.		75	
	Accounts Payable			75
	(b)			
	Wages Expense		125	
	Wages Payable			125
	(c)			
	Depreciation Expense – Equipment		100	
	Accumulated Depreciation – Equip-ment			100
	(d)			
	Rent Expense		500	
	Prepaid Rent			500
	(e)			
	Unearned Advertising Revenue		500	
	Other Revenue			500
	(f)			
	Prepaid Insurance*		525	
	Insurance Expense			525
	(g)			

*$900/12 months = $75/month; 5 months have been used (August 1 to December 31 = 5 months); therefore 7 months × $75/month = $525 remains unused.

PROBLEM 3–3

	General Journal			
Date	Account/Explanation	PR	Debit	Credit
	Interest Receivable		250	
	Interest Earned			250
	(a)			
	Insurance Expense		200	
	Prepaid Insurance			200
	(b)			
	Supplies Expense		200	
	Unused Supplies			200
	(c)			
	Interest Expense		25	
	Interest Payable			25
	(d)			
	Subscription Revenue		7,500	
	Unearned Subscription Revenue			7,500
	(e) ($9,000 × 5/6 mos. = $7,500)			
	Salaries Expense		300	
	Salaries Payable			300
	(f)			
	Prepaid Rent		300	
	Rent Expense			300
	(g)			
	Truck Operation Expense		400	
	Accounts Payable			400
	(h)			

PROBLEM 3–4

General Journal				
Date	Account/Explanation	PR	Debit	Credit
	Depreciation Expense – Truck		150	
	Accumulated Depreciation – Truck. . . .			150
	(a) ($6,000 × 6/48 mos. = $750 − 600 = $150)			
	(b) No Entry Required			
	Unused Supplies		300	
	Supplies Expense			300
	(c)			
	Rent Expense		400	
	Prepaid Rent			400
	(d)			
	Wages Expense		250	
	Wages Payable			250
	(e)			
	Interest Expense		200	
	Interest Payable			200
	(f) ($8,000 × 10% = $800 − 600 = $200)			
	Utilities Expense		150	
	Utilities Payable			150
	(g)			
	Insurance Expense		500	
	Prepaid Insurance.			500
	(h) ($1,200 × 1/12 mos. = $100 prepaid; $600 − 100 = $500)			
	Unearned Rent Revenue		600	
	Rent Earned			600
	(i)			
	Commissions Earned		2,000	
	Other Unearned Revenue.			2,000
	(j)			

PROBLEM 3–5

1., 3., 4., and 6.

Roth Contractors Corporation

Cash 101

(a) 5,000	(b) 1,200
(g) 800	(e) 1,800
(i) 2,000	(h) 3,450
(m) 2,000	(l) 3,225
Bal. 125	

Accounts Receivable 110

(f) 4,500	(i) 2,000
(j) 6,500	
Bal. 9,000	

Prepaid Insurance 161

(e) 1,800	(o) 150
Bal. 1,650	

Prepaid Rent 162

(b) 1,200	(p) 400
Bal. 800	

Supplies 173

(q) 350	

Truck 184

(c) 10,000	

Accounts Payable 210

	(c) 10,000
	(d) 1,000
	(n) 100
	Bal. 11,100

Wages Payable 237

	(s) 1,500

Unearned Revenue 249

	(r) 2,000

Accum. Dep'n Truck 194

	(t) 208

Share Capital 320

	(a) 5,000

Repair Revenue 450

(r) 2,000	(f) 4,500
	(g) 800
	(j) 6,500
	(m) 2,000
	Bal. 11,800

Advertising Expense 610

(h) 350	
(l) 200	
Bal. 550	

Depreciation Expense – Truck 624

(t) 208	

Insurance Expense 631

(o) 150	

Interest Expense 632

(h) 100	
(l) 150	
Bal. 250	

Rent Expense 654

(p) 400	

Supplies Expense 668

(d) 1,000	(q) 350
Bal. 650	

Telephone Expense 669

(h) 75	

Truck Operation Expense 670

(h) 425	
(l) 375	
Bal. 800	

Utilities Expense 676

(n) 100	

Wages Expense 677

(h) 2,500	
(l) 2,500	
(s) 1,500	
Bal. 6,500	

2.

Date	Account/Explanation	PR	Debit	Credit
	Cash		5,000	
	Share Capital			5,000
	(a)			
	Prepaid Rent		1,200	
	Cash			1,200
	(b)			
	Truck		10,000	
	Accounts Payable			10,000
	(c)			
	Supplies Expense		1,000	
	Accounts Payable			1,000
	(d)			
	Prepaid Insurance		1,800	
	Cash			1,800
	(e)			
	Accounts Receivable		4,500	
	Repair Revenue			4,500
	(f)			
	Cash		800	
	Repair Revenue			800
	(g)			
	Advertising Expense		350	
	Interest Expense		100	
	Telephone Expense		75	
	Truck Operation Expense		425	
	Wages Expense		2,500	
	Cash			3,450
	(h)			
	Cash		2,000	
	Accounts Receivable			2,000
	(i)			
	Accounts Receivable		6,500	
	Repair Revenue			6,500
	(j)			
	Advertising Expense		200	
	Interest Expense		150	
	Truck Operation Expense		375	
	Wages Expense		2,500	
	Cash			3,225
	(l)			
	Cash		2,000	
	Repair Revenue			2,000
	(m)			
	Utilities Expense		100	
	Accounts Payable			100
	(n)			

5.

General Journal				
Date	Account/Explanation	PR	Debit	Credit
	Insurance Expense		150	
	Prepaid Insurance			150
	(o)			
	Rent Expense		400	
	Prepaid Rent			400
	(p)			
	Supplies		350	
	Supplies Expense			350
	(q)			
	Repair Revenue		2,000	
	Unearned Revenue			2,000
	(r)			
	Wages Expense		1,500	
	Wages Payable			1,500
	(s)			
	Depreciation Expense – Truck		208	
	Accumulated Depreciation – Truck			208
	(t) $10,000/48 mos. = $208 per month*			

*Recall that depreciation is always rounded to the nearest whole dollar because it is not 'exact'; depreciation is based on estimated useful life and estimated residual value.

7.

Roth Contractors Corporation
Adjusted Trial Balance
December 31, 2015

	Account Balances	
	Debit	Credit
Cash	$ 125	
Accounts Receivable	9,000	
Prepaid Insurance	1,650	
Prepaid Rent	800	
Supplies	350	
Truck	10,000	
Accumulated Depreciation – Truck		$ 208
Accounts Payable		11,100
Wages Payable		1,500
Unearned Revenue		2,000
Share Capital		5,000
Repair Revenue		11,800
Advertising Expense	550	
Depreciation Expense – Truck	208	
Insurance Expense	150	
Interest Expense	250	
Rent Expense	400	
Supplies Expense	650	
Telephone Expense	75	
Truck Expense	800	
Utilities Expense	100	
Wages Expense	6,500	
Totals	$31,608	$31,608

PROBLEM 3–6

1. The general journal is as follows:

General Journal				
Date	Account/Explanation	PR	Debit	Credit
Dec. 31	Repair Revenue		11,800	
	Income Summary			11,800
	To close revenue account to income summary.			
31	Income Summary		9,683	
	Advertising Expense			550
	Depreciation Expense – Truck			208
	Insurance Expense			150
	Interest Expense			250
	Rent Expense			400
	Supplies Expense			650
	Telephone Expense			75
	Truck Expense			800
	Utilities Expense			100
	Wages Expense			6,500
	To close expense accounts to income summary.			
31	Income Summary		2,117	
	Retained Earnings			2,117
	To close net income in income summary to retained earnings.			

2. The post-closing trial balance is as follows:

Roth Contractors Corporation
Post-Closing Trial Balance
December 31, 2015

	Debits	Credits
Cash	$ 125	
Accounts receivable	9,000	
Prepaid insurance	1,650	
Prepaid rent	800	
Supplies	350	
Truck	10,000	
Accumulated depreciation – truck		$ 208
Accounts payable		11,100
Wages payable		1,500
Unearned revenue		2,000
Share capital		5,000
Retained earnings		2,117
Totals	$21,925	$21,925

PROBLEM 3–7

1., 3., 6., and 8.

Packer Corporation

Cash (101)
Debit	Credit
12,000	

Accounts Receivable (110)
Debit	Credit
3,600	

Prepaid Insurance (161)
Debit	Credit
(a) 900	
Bal. 900	

Supplies (173)
Debit	Credit
2,500	
(b) 350	
Bal. 2,850	

Land (180)
Debit	Credit
15,000	

Building (181)
Debit	Credit
60,000	

Furniture (182)
Debit	Credit
3,000	

Equipment (183)
Debit	Credit
20,000	

Accumulated Depreciation – Building (191)
Debit	Credit
	(c) 1,200

Accumulated Depreciation – Furniture (192)
Debit	Credit
	300
	(d) 300

Accumulated Depreciation – Equipment (193)
Debit	Credit
	(e) 1,000

Accounts Payable (210)
Debit	Credit
	4,400

Interest Payable (222)
Debit	Credit
	(f) 208

Salaries Payable (226)
Debit	Credit
	(i) 325

Unearned Commissions Revenue (242)
Debit	Credit
(g) 750	1,200
	Bal. 450

Unearned Subscriptions Revenue (250)
Debit	Credit
	800
	(h) 2,000
	Bal. 2,800

Bank Loan Long Term (271)
Debit	Credit
	47,600

Share Capital (320)
Debit	Credit
	52,100

Retained Earnings (340)
Debit	Credit
	(l) 6,967

Income Summary (360)
Debit	Credit
(k) 62,383	(j) 69,350
(l) 6,967	
	Bal. 0

Commissions Earned (410)
Debit	Credit
	37,900
	(g) 750
	Bal. 38,650
(j) 38,650	
	Bal. 0

Subscription Revenue (480)
Debit	Credit
(h) 2,000	32,700
	Bal. 30,700
(j) 30,700	
	Bal. 0

Advertising Expense (610)
Debit	Credit
4,300	(k) 4,300
Bal. 0	

Depreciation Expense – Building (621)
Debit	Credit
(c) 1,200	(k) 1,200
Bal. 0	

Depreciation Expense – Furniture (622)
Debit	Credit
(d) 300	(k) 300
Bal. 0	

Depreciation Expense Equipment (623)
Debit	Credit
(e) 1,000	(k) 1,000
Bal. 0	

Insurance Expense (631)
Debit	Credit
1,800	(a) 900
Bal. 900	(k) 900
Bal. 0	

Interest Expense (632)
Debit	Credit
2,365	
(f) 208	
Bal. 2,573	(k) 2,573
Bal. 0	

Salaries Expense (656)
Debit	Credit
33,475	
(i) 325	
Bal. 33,800	(k) 33,800
Bal. 0	

Supplies Expense (668)
Debit	Credit
15,800	(b) 350
Bal. 15,450	(k) 15,450
Bal. 0	

Utilities Expense (676)
Debit	Credit
2,860	(k) 2,860
Bal. 0	

2. Adjusting entries:

General Journal				
Date	Account/Explanation	PR	Debit	Credit
Aug. 31	Prepaid Insurance.......................		900	
	Insurance Expense...................			900
	(a) ($1,800 × 6/12 mos. = $900)			
31	Supplies..............................		350	
	Supplies Expense....................			350
	(b)			
31	Depreciation Expense – Building.........		1,200	
	Accumulated Depreciation – Building .			1,200
	(c) ($60,000 × 12/600 mos. = $1,200)			
31	Depreciation Expense – Furniture........		300	
	Accumulated Depreciation – Furniture			300
	(d) ($3,000 × 12/120 mos. = $300)			
31	Depreciation Expense – Equipment......		1,000	
	Accumulated Depreciation – Equipment................................			1,000
	(e) ($20,000 × 12/240 mos. = $1,000)			
31	Interest Expense.......................		208	
	Interest Payable.....................			208
	(f)			
31	Unearned Commissions Revenue........		750	
	Commissions Earned.................			750
	(g)			
31	Subscription Revenue..................		2,000	
	Unearned Subscriptions Revenue.....			2,000
	(h)			
31	Salaries Expense.......................		325	
	Salaries Payable....................			325
	(i)			

4. The adjusted trial balance is as follows:

Packer Corporation
Adjusted Trial Balance
August 31, 2015

| | Account Balances | |
	Debit	Credit
Cash	$ 12,000	
Accounts Receivable	3,600	
Prepaid Insurance	900	
Supplies	2,850	
Land	15,000	
Building	60,000	
Furniture	3,000	
Equipment	20,000	
Accumulated Depreciation – Building		$ 1,200
Accumulated Depreciation – Furniture		300
Accumulated Depreciation – Equipment		1,000
Accounts Payable		4,400
Interest Payable		208
Salaries Payable		325
Unearned Commissions Revenue		450
Unearned Subscriptions Revenue		2,800
Bank Loan- Long Term		47,600
Share Capital		52,100
Commissions Earned		38,650
Subscription Revenue		30,700
Advertising Expense	4,300	
Depreciation Expense – Building	1,200	
Depreciation Expense – Furniture	300	
Depreciation Expense – Equipment	1,000	
Insurance Expense	900	
Interest Expense	2,573	
Salaries Expense	33,800	
Supplies Expense	15,450	
Utilities Expense	2,860	
	$179,733	$179,733

5. The income statement, statement of changes in equity, and balance sheet are as follows:

Packer Corporation
Income Statement
For the Year Ended August 31, 2015

Revenue		
Commissions	$38,650	
Subscriptions	30,700	
Total Revenue		$69,350
Expenses		
Advertising	4,300	
Depreciation – Building	1,200	
Depreciation – Furniture	300	
Depreciation – Equipment	1,000	
Insurance	900	
Interest	2,573	
Salaries	33,800	
Supplies	15,450	
Utilities	2,860	
Total Expenses		62,383
Net Income		$ 6,967

Packer Corporation
Statement of Changes in Equity
For the Year Ended August 31, 2015

	Share Capital	Retained Earnings	Total Equity
Opening Balance	$ -0-	$ -0-	$ -0-
Shares Issued	52,100	-0-	52,100
Net Income	-0-	6,967	6,967
Ending Balance	$52,100	$6,967	$59,067

Packer Corporation
Balance Sheet
At August 31, 2015

Assets

Cash		$12,000
Accounts Receivable		3,600
Prepaid Insurance		900
Supplies		2,850
Land		15,000
Buildings	$60,000	
Less: Accum. Depreciation	1,200	58,800
Furniture	$3,000	
Less: Accum. Depreciation	300	2,700
Equipment	$20,000	
Less: Accum. Depreciation	1,000	19,000
Total Assets		$114,850

Liabilities

Accounts Payable		$4,400
Interest Payable		208
Salaries Payable		325
Unearned Advertising		450
Unearned Subscriptions		2,800
Bank Loan – Long-Term		47,600
Total Liabilities		55,783

Equity

Share Capital	$52,100	
Retained Earnings	6,967	
Total Equity		59,067
Total Liabilities and Equity		$114,850

6. Closing entries:

General Journal				
Date	Account/Explanation	PR	Debit	Credit
Aug. 31	Commissions Earned		38,650	
	Subscription Revenue		30,700	
	Income Summary			69,350
	(j)			
31	Income Summary		62,383	
	Advertising Expense.			4,300
	Depreciation Expense – Building			1,200
	Depreciation Expense – Furniture			300
	Depreciation Expense – Equipment . . .			1,000
	Insurance Expense			900
	Interest Expense			2,573
	Salaries Expense			33,800
	Supplies Expense			15,450
	Utilities Expense			2,860
	(k)			
31	Income Summary		6,967	
	Retained Earnings.			6,967
	(k)			

Note: The closing entries were posted into the T-accounts as (j), (k), and (l).

7. The post-closing trial balance:

Packer Corporation
Post-Closing Trial Balance
August 31, 2015

	Account Balances	
	Debit	Credit
Cash	$ 12,000	
Accounts Receivable	3,600	
Prepaid Insurance	900	
Unused Supplies	2,850	
Land	15,000	
Building	60,000	
Furniture	3,000	
Equipment	20,000	
Accumulated Depreciation – Building		$ 1,200
Accumulated Depreciation – Furniture		300
Accumulated Depreciation – Equipment		1,000
Accounts Payable		4,400
Interest Payable		208
Salaries Payable		325
Unearned Advertising Revenue		450
Unearned Subscriptions Revenue		2,800
Bank Loan – Long-Term		47,600
Share Capital		52,100
Retained Earnings		6,967
	$117,350	$117,350

Chapter 4 Solutions

PROBLEM 4–1

Norman Company Ltd.
Balance Sheet
At December 31, 2015

Assets

Current		
Cash	$250	
Accounts Receivable	138	
Notes Receivable	18	
Prepaid Insurance	12	
Unused Office Supplies	70	
Total Current Assets		$488
Property, Plant, and Equipment		
Land	115	
Building	400	
Equipment	140	
Net Property, Plant, and Equipment		655
Total Assets		$1,143

Liabilities

Current		
Accounts Payable	$125	
Bank Loan	110	
Salaries Payable	14	
Total Current Liabilities		$249
Non-current		
Mortgage Payable		280
Total Liabilities		529

Equity

Share Capital	400	
Retained Earnings	214	
Total Equity		614
Total Liabilities and Equity		$1,143

PROBLEM 4–2

1. Calculation of net income:

Revenue	$80,000
Salaries Expense	(39,000)
Depreciation	(1,100)
Interest	(1,300)
Income Taxes	(2,300)
Advertising	(7,200)
Insurance	(1,200)
Utilities	(3,600)
Telephone	(1,100)
Rent	(17,950)
Net Income	$5,250

2. The statement of changes in equity is as follows:

Dark Edge Sports Inc.
Statement of Changes in Equity
For the Year Ended December 31, 2015

	Share Capital	Retained Earnings	Total Equity
Opening Balance	$3,000	$2,000	$5,000
Net Income		5,250	5,250
Dividends		(600)	(600)
Ending Balance	$3,000	$6,650	$9,650

3. The balance sheet is as follows:

Dark Edge Sports Inc.
Balance Sheet
At December 31, 2015

Assets

Current

Cash		$1,500
Accounts Receivable		18,700
Prepaid Expenses (1,300 + 600)		1,900
Total Current Assets		22,100
Property, Plant, and Equipment Equipment	$12,500	
Less: Accumulated Depreciation	2,000	
Net Property, Plant, and Equipment		10,500
Total Assets		$32,600

Liabilities

Current

Bank Loan*	$10,000	
Accounts Payable	8,350	
Income Taxes Payable	4,600	
Total Current Liabilities		$22,950
Equity Share Capital	3,000	
Retained Earnings	6,650	
Total Equity		9,650
Total Liabilities and Equity		$32,600

*Alternately, with appropriate disclosure, "Borrowings"

4. Amount by which total current liabilities exceed total current assets:

Current Assets	$22,100
Current Liabilities	22,950
Difference	$ 850

5. After the $5,000 bank loan is received, both current assets and current liabilities will increase by the same amount (Debit to Cash; credit to Bank Loan). The difference will remain $850.

6. The company appears to have negative working capital (current assets less current liabilities) with or without the loan. More information should be requested, such as why the loan is needed. If it will be used to purchase a non-current asset like more equipment, perhaps the loan repayment terms should be extended by several years in which case the loan would be classified as a long-term liability causing working capital to be positive instead of negative as a result of the loan.

Chapter 5 Solutions

PROBLEM 5–1

1. The Salem Corp. general journal is as follows:

	General Journal			
Date	Account/Explanation	PR	Debit	Credit
Jul. 2	Cash...............................		5,000	
	Share Capital.......................			5,000
	To record the issue of common shares.			
2	Merchandise Inventory.................		3,500	
	Accounts Payable..................			3,500
	To record Purchases on credit 2/10, n/30, from Blic Pens, Ltd.			
2	Accounts Receivable..................		2,000	
	Sales..............................			2,000
	To record sale to Spellman Chair Rentals, Inc.; terms 2/10, n/30.			
	Cost of Goods Sold....................		1,200	
	Merchandise Inventory..............			1,200
	To record the cost of sales.			
3	Rent Expense.........................		500	
	Cash..............................			500
	To record July rent payment.			
5	Equipment............................		1,000	
	Cash..............................			1,000
	To record purchase of equipment.			
8	Cash.................................		200	
	Sales..............................			200
	To record cash sale to Ethan Matthews Furniture Ltd.			
	Cost of Goods Sold....................		120	
	Merchandise Inventory..............			120
	To record the cost of sales.			
8	Merchandise Inventory.................		2,000	
	Accounts Payable..................			2,000
	To record purchase of merchandise inventory; terms 2/15, n/30, from Shaw Distributors, Inc.			
9	Cash.................................		1,960	
	Sales Discount........................		40	
	Accounts Receivable...............			2,000
	To record receipt of amount due from Spellman Chair Rentals, Inc. less the discount.			
10	Accounts Payable.....................		3,500	
	Cash..............................			3,430
	Merchandise Inventory..............			70
	To record payment to Blic Pens Ltd. less the discount.			
10	Merchandise Inventory.................		200	
	Accounts Payable..................			200
	To record purchase of merchandise inventory from Peel Products, Inc.; terms n/30.			

	General Journal			
Date	Account/Explanation	PR	Debit	Credit
Jul. 15	Accounts Receivable		2,000	
	Sales			2,000
	To record sale to Eagle Products Corp. 2/10, n/30.			
	Cost of Goods Sold		1,300	
	Merchandise Inventory			1,300
	To record the cost of sales.			
15	Merchandise Inventory		1,500	
	Accounts Payable			1,500
	To record purchase of merchandise inventory from Bevan Door, Inc.; terms 2/10, n/30.			
15	Accounts Payable		100	
	Merchandise Inventory			100
	To record credit memo from Shaw Distributors, Inc.			
16	Sales Returns and Allowances		200	
	Accounts Receivable			200
	To record return of defective items sold to Eagle Products Corp.; inventory scrapped.			
20	Accounts Receivable		3,500	
	Sales			3,500
	To record sale to Aspen Promotions, Ltd. 2/10, n/30.			
	Cost of Goods Sold		2,700	
	Merchandise Inventory			2,700
	To record the cost of sales.			
20	Accounts Payable		950	
	Cash.			931
	Merchandise Inventory			19
	To record payment of half of the amount due to Shaw Distributors, Inc. less memo and less discount.			
24	Cash.		882	
	Sales Discounts		18	
	Accounts Receivable			900
	To record receipt of half of the amount due from Eagle Products Corp.; 2,000 − 200 return = 1,800/2 = 900.			
24	Accounts Payable		1,500	
	Cash.			1,470
	Merchandise Inventory			30
	To record payment made to Bevan Door, Inc. less discount.			
26	Accounts Receivable		600	
	Sales			600
	To record sale to Longbeach Sales, Ltd. for terms 2/10, n/30.			
	Cost of Goods Sold		400	
	Merchandise Inventory			400
	To record the cost of sales.			

General Journal				
Date	Account/Explanation	PR	Debit	Credit
Jul. 26	Merchandise Inventory		800	
	Accounts Payable			800
	To record purchase from Silverman Co. for terms 2/10, n/30.			
31	Merchandise Inventory		350	
	Cash.			350
	To record payment to Speedy Transport Co. for July transport of inventory to warehouse.			

2. The unadjusted ending balance in merchandise inventory is as follows:

Merchandise Inventory

2-Jul	3,500	1,200	2-Jul
8-Jul	2,000	120	8-Jul
10-Jul	200	70	10-Jul
15-Jul	1,500	1,300	15-Jul
26-Jul	800	100	15-Jul
31-Jul	350	2,700	20-Jul
		19	20-Jul
		30	24-Jul
		400	26-Jul
Unadj. Bal.	2,411		

3. The general journal entry is as follows:

General Journal				
Date	Account/Explanation	PR	Debit	Credit
July 31	Cost of Goods Sold		11	
	Merchandise Inventory			11
	To record adjustment to merchandise inventory calculated as $2,411 − $2,400 = $11.			

PROBLEM 5–2

Sales	$37,800
Less: Sales Returns and Allowances	690
Sales Discounts	310
Net Sales	$36,800
Cost of Goods Sold	26,800
Gross Profit	$10,000

PROBLEM 5–3

1. The income statement and statement of changes in equity are as follows:

Acme Automotive Inc.
Income Statement
Year Ended December 31, 2015

Sales			$310,000
Less: Sales returns and allowances		$2,900	
Sales discounts		1,300	4,200
Net sales			$305,800
Cost of goods sold			126,000
Gross profit			$179,800
Operating expenses:			
Selling expenses:			
Advertising expense	$14,000		
Commissions expense	29,000		
Delivery expense	14,800		
Rent expense	19,440		
Sales salaries expense	26,400		
Total selling expenses		$103,640	
General and administrative expenses:			
Depreciation expense	$12,000		
Insurance expense	10,400		
Office supplies expense	3,100		
Rent expense	12,960		
Telephone expense	1,800		
Utilities expense	4,200		
Wages expense – office	14,300		
Total general and administrative expenses		58,760	
Total operating expenses			162,400
Income from operations			$17,400
Other revenues and expenses:			
Rent revenue		$19,200	
Interest expense		(840)	18,360
Income before tax			$35,760
Income tax expense			4,200
Net income			$31,560

Acme Automotive Inc.
Statement of Changes in Equity
Year Ended December 31, 2015

	Share Capital	Retained Earnings	Total Equity
Opening balance	$50,000	$12,440	$62,440
Shares issued	20,000		20,000
Net income		31,560	31,560
Dividends		(11,000)	(11,000)
Ending balance	$70,000	$33,000	$103,000

2. Closing entries:

	General Journal			
Date	Account/Explanation	PR	Debit	Credit
Dec. 31	Sales.................................		310,000	
	Rent Sales............................		19,200	
	Income Summary....................			329,200
	(to close credit balance temporary accounts)			
31	Income Summary......................		297,640	
	Sales Returns and Allowances.........			2,900
	Sales Discounts.....................			1,300
	Cost of Goods Sold..................			126,000
	Advertising Expense.................			14,000
	Commissions Expense................			29,000
	Delivery Expense....................			14,800
	Rent Expense.......................			32,400
	Sales Salaries Expense...............			26,400
	Depreciation Expense................			12,000
	Insurance Expense...................			10,400
	Office Supplies Expense..............			3,100
	Telephone Expense..................			1,800
	Utilities Expense....................			4,200
	Wages Expense – Office..............			14,300
	Interest Expense....................			840
	Income Tax Expense.................			4,200
	(to close debit balance temporary accounts)			
31	Income Summary......................		31,560	
	Retained Earnings...................			31,560
	(to close Income Summary to Retained Earnings)			
31	Retained Earnings.....................		11,000	
	Dividends..........................			11,000
	(to close Dividends to Retained Earnings)			

Chapter 6 Solutions

PROBLEM 6–1

1. Weighted Average Cost Flow Assumption:

Product A

Date		Units	Unit Cost	COGS	Units	Unit Cost	Total Cost
		Purchased (Sold)			**Balance**		
Jan. 1	Opening Inventory				4,000 ×	$11.90 =	$47,600
Jan. 7	Purchase #1	8,000 ×	$12.00		12,000 ×	11.97^1 =	143,600
Mar. 30	Sale #1	(9,000) ×	11.97 =	($107,730)	3,000 ×	=	35,870
May 10	Purchase #2	12,000 ×	12.10		15,000 ×	12.07^2 =	181,070
Jul. 4	Sale #2	(14,000) ×	12.07 =	(168,980)	1,000 ×	=	**$12,090**

^{1}[$47,600 + (8,000 × $12)]/(4,000 + 8,000) = $11.97/unit (rounded)

^{2}[$35,870 + (12,000 × $12.10)]/(3,000 + 12,000) = $12.07/unit (rounded)

Product B

Date		Units	Unit Cost	COGS	Units	Unit Cost	Total Cost
		Purchased (Sold)			**Balance**		
Jan. 1	Opening Inventory				2,000 ×	$13.26 =	$26,520
Jan. 13	Purchase #1	5,000 ×	$13.81		7,000 ×	13.65^3 =	95,570
Jul. 15	Sale #1	(1,000) ×	13.65 =	($13,650)	6,000 ×	=	81,920
May 10	Purchase #2	7,000 ×	14.21		13,000 ×	13.95^4 =	181,390
Dec. 14	Sale #2	(8,000) ×	13.95 =	(111,600)	5,000 ×	=	**$69,790**

^{3}[$26,520 + (5,000 × $13.81)]/(2,000 + 5,000) = $13.65/unit (rounded)

^{4}[$81,920 + (7,000 × $14.21)]/(6,000 + 7,000) = $13.95/unit (rounded)

2. Total ending inventory at December 31, 2020:

Product A	$12,090
Product B	69,790
Total	$81,880

3. Gross profit percentage earned:

	Product A		Product B
Mar. 30 Sale	144,000	Jul. 15 Sale	20,000
Jul. 04 Sale	238,000	Dec. 14 Sale	168,000
Total Sales	382,000	Total Sales	188,000
COGS	276,710	COGS	125,250
Gross Profit	105,290	Gross Profit	62,750
Gross Profit %	27.56	Gross Profit %	33.38

PROBLEM 6–2

1. Ending inventory for 2016 was overstated by $2,000. Thus, cost of goods sold should have been $2,000 higher, or $22,000 and gross profit $2,000 lower, or $28,000. Because of this mistake, the 2017 opening inventory was also overstated by $2,000, causing cost of goods sold to be overstated by $2,000 and gross profit to be understated by $2,000. Gross profit should have been $29,000.

2. 2016 total and net assets were overstated by $2,000. 2017 total assets and net assets were correct.

PROBLEM 6–3

	2017			2018		
	Cost	Market	Unit Basis (LCNRV)	Cost	Market	Unit Basis (LCNRV)
Product X	$14,000	$15,000	$14,000	$15,000	$16,000	$15,000
Product Y	12,500	12,000	12,000	12,000	11,500	11,500
Product Z	11,000	11,500	11,000	10,500	10,000	10,000
Total	$37,500	$38,500	$37,000	$37,500	$37,500	$36,500

Chapter 7 Solutions

PROBLEM 7–1

a	The company has received a $3,000 loan from the bank, that was deposited into its bank account but was not recorded in the books of the company.
e	A $250 cheque was not returned with the bank statement though it was paid by the bank.
d	Cheques amounting to $4,290 shown as outstanding on the November reconciliation still have not been returned by the bank.
a	A collection of a note receivable for $1,000 made by the bank has not been previously reported to Goertzen. This includes interest earned of $50.
c	The bank has erroneously charged Goertzen with an $1,100 cheque which should have been charged to Gagetown Ltd.
b	A $350 cheque made out by Fynn Company and deposited by Goertzen has been returned by the bank marked NSF; this is the first knowledge Goertzen has of this action.
a	A cheque for $840 was erroneously recorded as $730 in the company records.
c	A $600 bank deposit of December 31 does not appear on the bank statement.
b	Bank service charges amounting to $75 were deducted from the bank statement but not yet from the company records.

PROBLEM 7–2

1. (a) Entry to record the write-off of $25,000:

General Journal				
Date	Account/Explanation	PR	Debit	Credit
	Allowance for Doubtful Accounts		25,000	
	Accounts Receivable			25,000

(b) Entry to record the recovery of $15,000:

General Journal				
Date	Account/Explanation	PR	Debit	Credit
	Accounts Receivable		15,000	
	Allowance for Doubtful Accounts			15,000
	Cash		15,000	
	Accounts Receivable			15,000

2. Allowance for doubtful accounts = ($15,000 Cr. − $25,000 Dr.) (1a) + $15,000 Cr. (1b) = $5,000 Cr. balance

3. (a) The entries required for bad debts based on three per cent of credit sales:

Balance required = 3% of credit sales
                  = 3% × 70% × $1,000,000
                  = $21,000

General Journal					
Date	Account/Explanation		PR	Debit	Credit
	Bad Debt Expense......................			21,000	
	Allowance for Doubtful Accounts.....				21,000
	To record bad debts using % of sales, the income statement method.				

General Journal					
Date	Account/Explanation		PR	Debit	Credit
	Bad Debt Expense......................			7,500	
	Allowance for Doubtful Accounts.....				7,500
	To record bad debts using simplified balance sheet approach: 5% of receivables (250,000 × 5% = 12,500 required balance − 5,000 unadjusted balance = 7,500 required adjustment).				

(b)

(c) Calculation of uncollectible amount at December 31, 2012:

Age (days)	Accounts Receivable	Estimated Loss Percentage	Estimated Uncollectible Amount
1-30	$100,000	2%	$2,000
31-60	50,000	4%	2,000
61-90	25,000	5%	1,250
91-120	60,000	10%	6,000
Over 120	15,000	50%	7,500
	$250,000		$18,750

General Journal					
Date	Account/Explanation		PR	Debit	Credit
	Bad Debt Expense......................			13,750	
	Allowance for Doubtful Accounts.....				13,750
	To record bad debts using aging analysis, a balance sheet approach (18,750 required balance − 5,000 unadjusted balance = 13,750 required adjustment).				

4. (a) December 31, 2018 adjusted AFDA balance = $26,000 (calculated as 5,000 unadjusted balance + 21,000 adjustment)

    (b) December 31, 2018 adjusted AFDA balance = $12,500 (calculated as 5,000 unadjusted balance + 7,500 adjustment)

    (c) December 31, 2018 adjusted AFDA balance = $18,750 (calculated as 5,000 unadjusted balance + 13,750 adjustment)

Chapter 8 Solutions

PROBLEM 8–1

Cost of Lots:

Cheque to Jones		$140,000
Bank loan assumed by Arrow		100,000
Razing of barns		6,000
Legal, accounting, and brokerage Fees		20,000
Clearing and levelling costs		10,000
Total outlays		$276,000
Less: Contra items:		
Proceeds from crops	$6,000	
Proceeds from house	1,600	
Proceeds from lumber	4,400	12,000
Net cost of 500 lots		$264,000
Net cost per lot ($264,000/500 lots)		$528

PROBLEM 8–2

1. Depreciation expense for each of 2019 through to 2022 inclusive:

$$\text{Depreciation/unit} = \frac{\text{Cost} - \text{Residual}}{\text{Expected Total Production}} = \frac{\$95,000 - \$5,000}{9,000 \text{ units}} = \$10/\text{unit}$$

Year	Actual Units Produced	Depreciation Expense	Calculations
2019	2,000	$20,000	2,000 units × $10/unit = 20,000
2020	3,000	30,000	3,000 units × $10/unit = 30,000
2021	2,800	28,000	2,800 units × $10/unit = 28,000
2022	2,900	12,000	1,200 units × $10/unit = 12,000*
		$90,000	Total depreciation

* Maximum allowable total depreciation is Cost-Residual or $90,000. This is based on a total of 9,000 units. Therefore, the maximum amount of depreciation that can be recorded in 2022 is $12,000 which is based on 1,200 units.

2. Accumulated depreciation at the end of 2022 is $90,000.

3. Carrying amount of the machine at the end of 2022 is $5,000 ($95,000 − 90,000).

4. Entry on January 15, 2023 to record the sale of the machinery for $12,000:

General Journal					
Date	Account/Explanation	PR	Debit	Credit
	Cash.................................		12,000	
	Accumulated Depreciation..............		90,000	
	Machinery.........................			95,000
	Gain on Disposal....................			7,000
	To record gain on disposal calculated as: [$95,000 Cost of Machinery − $90,000 Accumulated Depreciation = $5,000 Carrying Amount (or net book value)] − $12,000 Proceeds of Disposal = $(7,000)			

Chapter 9 Solutions

PROBLEM 9–1

1. (a) Entry to record receipt of loan proceeds from the bank:

General Journal					
Date	Account/Explanation	PR	Debit	Credit
Dec. 31	Cash................................		100,000	
	Loan Payable......................			100,000
	To record loan from First National Bank.			

(b) Entry to record purchase of the equipment:

General Journal				
Date	Account/Explanation	PR	Debit	Credit
Jan. 2	Equipment		95,000	
	Cash...............................			95,000
	To record purchase of equipment.			

2. The loan repayment schedule is as follows:

Zinc Corp.
Loan Repayment Schedule

	A	B	C	D	E
			(D − B)		(A − C)
Year Ended Dec. 31	Beginning Loan Balance	(A × 8%) Interest Expense	Reduction of Loan Payable	Total Loan Payment	Ending Loan Balance
2016	$100,000	$8,000	$22,192	$30,192	$77,808
2017	77,808	6,225	23,967	30,192	53,841
2018	53,841	4,307	25,885	30,192	27,956
2019	27,956	2,236	27,956	30,192	-0-

3. Entry to record the last loan payment:

General Journal				
Date	Account/Explanation	PR	Debit	Credit
Dec. 31	Interest Expense		2,236	
	Loan Payable		27,956	
	Cash...............................			30,192
	To record final loan payment to First National Bank.			

4. The partial balance sheet is as follows:

Zinc Corp.
Partial Balance Sheet
At December 31, 2017

Liabilities

Current
 Current Portion of First National Bank Loan
  (Note X) $25,885
Non-current
 First National Bank Loan (Note X)   27,956

Note X would disclose pertinent information including details of the loan
repayment agreement (for example, interest rate, repayment terms, security)
if just the carry amount is shown on the balance sheet as above.

Chapter 10 Solutions

PROBLEM 10–1

1. The equity section of the balance sheet after the split is as follows:

Before split	**After split**
Equity	*Equity*
Common Shares	Common Shares
Authorized – 5,000 Shares	Authorized – 5,000 Shares
Issued and Outstanding – 1,000 Shares $100,000	Issued and Outstanding – 5,000 Shares $100,000

2. Memorandum indicating the new number of shares:

General Journal					
Date	Account/Explanation	PR	Debit	Credit
	Memorandum			
	The outstanding shares were increased			
	from 1,000 to 5,000 by a 5-for-1 share split.			

3. It can be estimated that the market price per share would approximate $8 ($40/5). However, the share split should not have any effect on the overall value of the firm to investors.
   Therefore, if five times as many shares are now outstanding, each share should be worth
   1/5 as much but each shareholder's paid-in capital would be the same before and after the
   share split.

PROBLEM 10–2

1. General journal to record 2019 transactions:

Date	Account/Explanation	PR	Debit	Credit
	General Journal			
Feb. 15	Cash Dividends Declared*		112	
	Dividends Payable – Preferred Shares .			12
	Dividends Payable – Common Shares .			100
Apr. 1	Dividends Payable – Preferred Shares		12	
	Dividends Payable – Common Shares		100	
	Cash			112
May 1	Share Dividends Declared*		400	
	Share Dividends to be Distributed			400
	(2,000 shares × 10% = 200 shares × $2)			
Jun. 15	Share Dividends to be Distributed		400	
	Common Shares			400
Aug. 15	Cash Dividends Declared*		122	
	Dividends Payable – Preferred Shares .			12
	Dividends Payable – Common Shares			110
	(2,200 shares × $0.05)			
Oct. 1	Dividends Payable – Preferred Shares		12	
	Dividends Payable – Common Shares		110	
	Cash			122
Dec. 15	Share Dividends Declared*		660	
	Share Dividends to be Distributed			660
	(2,200 shares × 10% × $3 = $660)			
27	Share Dividends to be Distributed		660	
	Common Shares			660
31	Income Summary		1,400	
	Retained Earnings			1,400
31	Retained Earnings**		1,294	
	Share Dividends Declared			1,060
	Cash Dividends Declared			234

* Alternatively, Retained Earnings could have been debited.

**If Retained Earnings was debited on the dividend declaration dates, then a closing entry is not required.

2. The statement of changes is as follows:

TWR Contracting Inc.
Statement of Changes in Equity
For the Year Ended December 31, 2019

	Share Capital		Retained Earnings	Total Equity
	Common	Preferred		
Opening Balance	$2,000	$400	$ 900	$ 3,300
Net Income			1,400	1,400
Dividends Declared				
Cash			(234)	(234)
Common Shares	1,060		(1,060)	
Ending Balance	$3,060	$400	$ 1,006	$ 4,466

PROBLEM 10–3

1. General journal to record 2019 transactions:

	General Journal			
Date	Account/Explanation	PR	Debit	Credit
Feb. 10	Cash Dividends Declared*		32,000	
	Dividends Payable – Preferred Shares .			30,000
	Dividends Payable – Common Shares .			2,000
	To record dividend declaration; $15,000 in arrears to Preferred + $15,000 to Preferred for 2019 leaves remainder of $2,000 for Common.			
Mar. 1	Dividends Payable – Preferred Shares		30,000	
	Dividends Payable – Common Shares		2,000	
	Cash			32,000
	To record payment of dividends declared February 10.			
5	Cash		36,000	
	Preferred Shares			36,000
	To record issuance of 2,000 preferred shares at $18 each.			
	Memorandum Entry: Board of Directors declared a 2:1 split on preferred and common shares:			
	Preferred Shares – (30,000 shares + 2,000 shares) × 2 = 64,000			
	Common Shares – 70,000 × 2 = 140,000			
Jun. 22	Cash		80,000	
	Common Shares			80,000
	To record issuance of 20,000 common shares at $4 each.			
Nov. 10	Share Dividends Declared*		112,000	
	Share Dividends to be Distributed			112,000
	To record share dividend; [20% × (140,000 + 20,000)] × $3.50.			
Dec. 15	Share Dividends to be Distributed		112,000	
	Common Shares			112,000
	To record distribution of common share dividend.			
31	Income Summary		290,000	
	Retained Earnings			290,000
	To close the credit balance in the Income Summary account.			
31	Retained Earnings**		144,000	
	Cash Dividends Declared			32,000
	Share Dividends Declared			112,000
	To close the dividend accounts.			

* Alternatively, Retained Earnings could have been debited.

** If Retained Earnings was debited on the dividend declaration dates, then a closing entry is not required.

2. The equity section of the balance sheet is as follows:

Wondra Inc.
Partial Balance Sheet
December 31, 2019

Contributed Capital	
Preferred Shares; $0.50 cumulative; unlimited shares authorized; 64,000 shares issued and outstanding	$516,000
Common Shares; unlimited shares authorized; 192,000 shares issued and outstanding	752,000
Total contributed capital	$1,268,000
Retained Earnings	241,000
Total Equity	$1,509,000

Part 2 Calculations (using T-accounts to track changing account balances):

Preferred Shares

$480,000	(30,000 shares)	Dec. 31/18 balance
36,000	(2,000 shares)	Mar. 5/19
0	(32,000 shares)	Apr. 15/19
$516,000	(64,000 shares)	Dec. 31/19 balance

Common Shares

$560,000	(70,000 shares)	Dec. 31/18 balance
0	(70,000 shares)	Apr. 15/19
80,000	(20,000 shares)	Jun. 22/19
112,000	(32,000 shares)	Nov. 15/19
$752,000	(192,000 shares)	Dec. 31/19 balance

Retained Earnings

		$95,000	Dec. 31/18 balance
Dec. 31/19 { Cash Div.	32,000		
Share Div.	112,000		
		290,000	Dec. 31/19
		241,000	Dec. 31/19 balance

PROBLEM 10–4

1. The paid-in capital per common share, and book value per common share are:

$$\text{Paid-in capital per common share} = \frac{\text{Total Paid-in Capital}}{\text{Number of shares outstanding}}$$

$$= \$3,070/300 = \$10.23 \text{ (rounded)}$$

$$\text{Book value per common share} = \frac{\text{Total equity}}{\text{Number of shares outstanding}}$$
$$= \$3{,}570/300 = \$11.90$$

2. There is little relationship between market price and the book value of a share. Book value provides only a basis on which to compare two or more companies, or to compare a company's market price per share. Market value is affected by investors' perceptions of future earnings expectations of the company. Also some assets recorded at historical cost, such as land, may have appreciated in value. This appreciation would be reflected in the market value of the common shares, but not in the book value.

Chapter 11 Solutions

PROBLEM 11–1

1. Entry to record the disposal:

	General Journal			
Date	Account/Explanation	PR	Debit	Credit
	Accumulated Depreciation..............		16^1	
	Cash..................................		12	
	Equipment.......................			20
	Gain on Sale of Equipment...........			8

Cost (given)	20
^{1}Acc. Depreciation (derived)	(16)
Book Value or Carrying Amount (given)	4
Cash Proceeds (given)	(12)
Gain on Sale (given)	8

Cash is increased by $12, the amount of the sale proceeds, but this does not represent cash flow from an operating activity. The sale of property, plant and equipment assets is an investing activity, and so will not be shown in the calculation of cash flow from operating activities. The $12 inflow of cash from the sale of the equipment will be shown as a cash inflow in the Investing Activities section of the SCF.

The $8 gain on sale is included in the calculation of net income. Since it (a) does not represent actual cash inflow (the $12 is the actual cash inflow) and (b) is not an operating activity, the gain is deducted from net income on the SCF to derive cash flow from operating activities.

2. Cash flow from operating activities calculated as follows:

Net Income	$33
Items Not Affecting Cash Flow	
Depreciation Expense	10
Gain on Sale of Equipment	(8)
Cash Flow from Operating Activities	$35

PROBLEM 11–2

1. Beginning retained earnings + net income − dividends declared = Ending retained earnings; 156 + 50 − 0 = 206. No dividends were declared so the net change in retained earnings of 50 is entirely an operating activity − net income.

2. The cash flow from operating activities is calculating as follows:

	Balance		Change		Cash Effect		Activity
	2019	2018					
	Dr. (Cr.)	Dr. (Cr.)	Dr.	Cr.	Inflow	Outflow	
Cash	100	86	14		To be explained		C&CE
Accounts Receivable	60	40	20			20	Operating
Inventory	36	30	6			6	Operating
Prepaid Rent	10	-0-	10			10	Operating
Retained Earnings	(206)	(156)		50	50		Operating
	-0-	-0-	50	50	50	36	

$14 net cash inflow

Cash flow from operating activities would be calculated as:

Net Income		$ 50
Adjustments to reconcile net income to cash provided by operating activities:		
Increase in Accounts Receivable	(20)	
Increase in Inventory	(6)	
Increase in Prepaid Rent	(10)	(36)
Cash Flow from operating activities		$ 14

PROBLEM 11–3

1. Entry to record the depreciation expense for the year:

General Journal					
Date	Account/Explanation	PR	Debit	Credit
	Depreciation Expense		100	
	Accumulated Depreciation – Machin-ery			100

There is no cash effect. However, the depreciation expense should be added back to the net loss figure when deriving cash flow from operating activities because it is a non-cash expense.

2. Entry to account for the change in the Machinery balance sheet account:

General Journal					
Date	Account/Explanation	PR	Debit	Credit
	Machinery		300	
	Cash.			300

Since (a) the Machinery account increased $300 (500 – 200) during the year, (b) no disposals occurred, and (c) all purchases of machinery were paid in cash, $300 of cash must have been spent on machinery purchases. This cash outflow is an investing activity.

3. Cash flow table:

	Balance		Change		Cash Effect		Activity
	2019	2018					
	Dr. (Cr.)	Dr. (Cr.)	Dr.	Cr.	Inflow	Outflow	
Cash	350	650		300	To be explained		C&CE
Machinery	500	200	300			300	Investing
Accumulated Depreciation	(250)	(150)		100	100		Operating
Retained Earnings	(600)	(700)	100			100	Operating
	-0-	-0-	400	400	100	400	

$300 net cash outflow

Statement of Cash Flows
For the Year Ended December 31, 2019

Cash flows from operating activities:	
Net Loss	$(100)
Adjustments to reconcile net loss to cash	
provided by operating activities	
Depreciation Expense	100
Net cash flow from operating activities	-0-
Cash flows from investing activities:	
Purchase of Machinery	(300)
Net decrease in cash	(300)
Cash at beginning of year	650
Cash at end of year	$350

PROBLEM 11–4

1. Cash flow table:

	Balance		Change		Cash Effect		Activity
	2019	2018					
	Dr. (Cr.)	Dr. (Cr.)	Dr.	Cr.	Inflow	Outflow	
Cash	1,350	1,800		*450	To be explained		C&CE
Borrowings	(800)	(1,300)	500			500	Financing
Retained Earnings	(550)	(500)		50	90		Operating
						40	Financing
	-0-	-0-	500	500	90	540	

*$450 net cash outflow

Cash flow from operating activities equals net income of $90. All revenue was received in cash and all expenses were paid in cash, and there were no changes to any other balance sheet accounts that affect cash flow from operating activities.

2. Dividends declared must have been $40, calculated as follows:

Opening Retained Earnings (given)	$500
Add: Net Income (given)	90
Less: Dividends Paid (derived)	**(40)**
Ending Retained Earnings (given)	$550

3. Cash Used by Financing Activities:

Repayment of Borrowings	$(500)
Payment of Dividends	(40)
	$(540)

PROBLEM 11–5

Calculations:

	Change		Cash Effect		Activity
	Dr.	Cr.	Inflow	Outflow	
Cash	*1,175		To be explained		C&CE
Accum. Dep'n.		120(b)	120		Operating
Accounts Receivable	(d)40			40	Operating
Merchandise Inventory		50(e)	50		Operating
Accum. Amort – Patents		5(f)	5		Operating
Wages Payable		20(c)	20		Operating
Borrowings	(g)250			250	Financing
Common Shares		500(h)	500		Financing
Retained Earnings		800(a)	800		Operating
	(i)30			30	Financing
	1,495	1,495	1,495	320	

*$1,175 net cash inflow

Dunn Corporation
Statement of Cash Flows
For the Year Ended December 31, 2019

Cash flows from operating activities:

Net Income		$800
Adjustments to reconcile net income to cash provided by operating activities		
Increase in accounts receivable		(40)
Decrease in merchandise inventory		50
Increase in wages payable		20
Depreciation and Amortization Expense ($120 + 5)		125
Net cash inflow from operating activities		955
Cash flows from financing activities:		
Repayment of borrowings	$(250)	
Common shares issued	500	
Payment of dividends	(30)	
Net cash inflow from financing activities		220
Net increase in cash		1,175
Cash at beginning of year**		25
Cash at End of Year		$1,200

**If the company had $1,200 cash on hand at the end of the year and cash increased by $1,175 during the year, cash on hand at the beginning of the year must be $25.

PROBLEM 11–6

Calculations:

	Change		Cash Effect		Activity
	Dr.	Cr.	Inflow	Outflow	
Cash	37,900[2]		To be explained		C&CE
Accounts Receivable	(c) 900			900	Operating
Merchandise Inventory		(d) 1,200	1,200		Operating
Equipment	(h) 10,000[5]				Investing
		(j) 15,000	(i)6,000[3]		Investing
			(j)1,500		Operating
Accum. Dep'n. – Equip.	(j) 7,500	(a) 3,000	3,000		Operating
Accum. Amort – Patents		(e) 100	100		Operating
Accounts Payable	(k) 1,000			1,000	Operating
Wages Payable		(b) 500	500		Operating
Dividends Payable		(i) 5,000[4]			
Borrowings	(f) 5,000			5,000	Financing
Common Shares		(g) 12,500	12,500		Financing
		(h) 10,000[5]			
Retained Earnings		20,000[1]	20,000		Operating
	(i) 5,000[4]				
	67,300	67,300	44,800	6,900	

$37,900^2$ net cash inflow

[1] Net income = $95,000 − 70,000 − 5,000 = $20,000

[2] Given

[3] Cost of machinery	$15,000
Accumulated depreciation (1/2)	(7,500)
Carrying amount	7,500
Cash proceeds	(6,000)
Loss on disposal	$1,500

The journal entry to record the sale would be:

	General Journal				
Date	Account/Explanation	PR	Debit	Credit
	Cash		6,000 (i)	
	Accumulated Dep'n.....................		7,500	
	Loss on Sale		1,500(j)	
	Machinery			15,000

Items (a) and (b) affect the SCF. The first (i) is a cash inflow from investing activities. The second (j) is added back to net income to arrive at cash flow from operating activities.

[4] Dividends were declared but not paid therefore there is no impact on cash.

[5] $10,000 of equipment was acquired by issuing common shares which is a non-cash transaction reported in a note but not included on the statement of cash flows.

1. The statement of cash flows is as follows:

Wheaton Co. Ltd.
Statement of Cash Flows
For the Year Ended December 31, 2019

Cash flows from operating activities:		
Net income ($95,000 − 70,000 − 5,000)		$ 20,000
Adjustments to reconcile net income to cash provided by operating activities:		
Depreciation and amortization ($3,000 + 100)		3,100
Loss on Disposal of Machinery		1,500
Increase in wages payable		500
Increase in accounts receivable		(900)
Decrease in merchandise inventory		1,200
Decrease in accounts payable		(1,000)
Net cash inflow from operating activities		24,400
Cash flows from investing activities:		
Proceeds from sale of machinery	$ 6,000	
Net cash inflow from investing activities		6,000
Cash flows from financing activities:		
Repayment of borrowings	(5,000)	
Common shares issued for cash	12,500	
Net cash inflow from financing activities		7,500
Net Increase in cash (given)		37,900
Cash at beginning of year (given)		1,000
Cash at end of year (derived)		$ 38,900

2. The statement of cash flows shows that the company has financed its activities internally from operations and by issuing common shares. The sale of machinery also generated cash. It has repaid some borrowings and acquired some property, plant and equipment assets. Wheaton Co. Ltd. has generated substantially more cash than it has used in 2019.

Chapter 12 Solutions

PROBLEM 12–1

Belafonte Corporation
Balance Sheet
At April 30, 2011

Assets			Liabilities and Equity		
Cash	$ 2,000	(c)	Accounts Payable	$ 8,000	(f)
Accounts Receivable	8,000	(a)	Bonds Payable	20,000	(b)
Merchandise Inventories	20,000	(b)	Common Shares	15,000	(g)
Total Current Assets	30,000	(d)	Retained Earnings	7,000	(i)
Property, plant and equipment assets (net)	20,000	(b)			
			Total Liabilities and		
Total Assets	$50,000	(e)	Equity	$50,000	(h)

Information:

(1) Current assets = 3.75 × Current liabilities (accounts payable)

(2) Sales for year = $73,000

(3) Merchandise inventories = $20,000 = Property, plant and equipment assets = bonds payable

(4) Accounts receivable collection period = 40 days

$$\frac{\text{Average accounts receivable}}{\text{Net credit sales}} \times 365 \text{ days}$$

(5) Bonds payable = 10 × cash

(6) Total current assets = 2 × common shares.

Calculations:

(a) $\dfrac{\text{Average accounts receivable}}{\$73,000} \times 365 \text{ days} = 40 \text{ days}$

Average accounts receivable = $8,000

(b) Merchandise inventory, property, plant and equipment assets (net), and bonds payable each equal $20,000

(c) Cash = bonds payable/10 = $20,000/10 = $2,000

(d) Total current assets = $2,000 + 8,000 + 20,000 = $30,000

(e) Total assets = $20,000 + 30,000 = $50,000

(f) Accounts payable = Current assets/3.75 = $30,000/3.75 = $8,000

(g) Common shares = Current assets/2 = $30,000/2 = $15,000

(h) Total liabilities and equity must equal total assets

(i) Retained earnings = Total liabilities and equity − accounts payable − bonds payable − common shares = $50,000 − 8,000 − 20,000 − $15,000 = $7,000

PROBLEM 12–2

Hook Limited
Balance Sheet
At December 31, 2011

Assets

Current

Cash		$ 30,000	
Accounts Receivable		150,000	(3)
Merchandise Inventories		90,000	(4)
Total Current Assets		270,000	(2)
Property, Plant, and Equipment	442,500 (10)		
Less: Accumulated Depreciation	100,000	342,500	(9)
Total Assets		$612,500	(8)

Liabilities

Current

Accounts Payable	$ 50,000		
Accrued Liabilities	70,000 (1)		
Total Current Liabilities		120,000	
Non-current			
8% Bonds Payable		125,000	(6)
		245,000	

Equity

Common Shares	80,000 (5)		
Retained Earnings	287,500 (12)	367,500	
Total Liabilities and Equity		$612,500	(11)

Calculations:

(1) Accrued liabilities = $120,000 − 50,000 = $70,000

(Total current liabilities − accounts payable)

(2) Total current assets = $120,000 + 150,000 = $270,000

(Total current liabilities + working capital)

(3) Accounts receivable = ($120,000 × 1.5) − 30,000 = $150,000

[(Total current liabilities × acid-test ratio) − cash]

(4) Inventories = $270,000 − 150,000 − 30,000 = $90,000

(Total current assets − accounts receivable − cash)

(5) Net income = [$80,000 − (80,000/8)] − $30,000 = $40,000

[Income before interest and income taxes − (income before interest and income taxes/times interest earned) − income taxes

Therefore, common shares = $40,000/5 × $10 = $80,000

(Net income/Earnings per share) × issued value

(6) Bonds payable = $80,000/8 divided by 0.08% = $125,000

[Income before interest and income taxes/Times interest earned)/Interest rate]

(7) If the ratio of equity to total assets is 0.60 to 1, then the ratio of liabilities to total assets is 0.40 to 1.

(8) Total assets = ($120,000 + 125,000)/0.4 = $612,500

[(Total current liabilities + total non-current liabilities)/Total debt to total assets ratio]

(9) Net PPE = $612,500 − 270,000 = $342,500

(Total assets − current assets)

(10) PPE = $342,500 + 100,000 = $442,500

(Net PPE + accumulated depreciation)

(11) Total liabilities and equity = Total assets = $612,500.

(12) Retained earnings = $612,500 − 245,000 − 80,000 = $287,500

(Total liabilities and equity − total liabilities − common shares)

Chapter 13 Solutions

PROBLEM 13–1

1. Schedule to allocate the 2015 net income to partners:

	Bog	Cog	Fog	Total
Profit to be allocated				$40,000
Interest allocation:				
Bog: $60,000 × 10%	$ 6,000			
Cog: $100,000 × 10%		$ 10,000		(18,000)
Fog: $20,000 × 10%			$ 2,000	
Balance				22,000
Salary allocation:	24,000	30,000	48,000	(102,000)
Balance (deficit)				(80,000)
Balance allocated in profit and loss sharing ratio:				
Bog: ($80,000) × 5/10	(40,000)			
Cog: ($80,000) × 3/10		(24,000)		80,000
Fog: ($80,000) × 2/10			(16,000)	
Balance				$ -0-
Total allocated to partners	($10,000)	$16,000	$34,000	

2. Entry to record the division of the 2015 net income:

General Journal				
Date	Account/Explanation	PR	Debit	Credit
	Income Summary		40,000	
	Bog, Capital		10,000	
	Cog, Capital			16,000
	Fog, Capital			34,000
	To record net income allocation to partners.			

Made in the USA
San Bernardino, CA
09 October 2018